A PLACE
TO BELONG

Letters from Catholic Women

Edited by Corynne Staresinic

auline
BOOKS & MEDIA

Library of Congress Control Number: 2020932769

CIP data is available.

ISBN-10: 0-8198-0870-9
ISBN-13: 978-0-8198-0870-7

Cover and interior design by Sr. Putri Madgalena Mamesah, FSP

Photos by Corynne and Nick Staresinic

The Catholic Women logo by Olivia Faye Co.

Published by Pauline Books & Media, 50 Saint Pauls Avenue, Boston, MA 02130-3491

Printed in the U.S.A.

www.pauline.org

Pauline Books & Media is the publishing house of the Daughters of St. Paul, an international congregation of women religious serving the Church with the communications media.

1 2 3 4 5 6 7 8 9   26 25 24 23 22 21

To Nick and Eloise

Contents

Letter from the Editor

Before I converted to Catholicism, upon discovering my interest in the Church, one of the common responses from my Evangelical loved ones was something like, "Corynne, how will you ever fit into the Catholic Church? That is where women go to be oppressed." As an eighteen-year-old woman who had only known a small handful of Catholics growing up and had only just started to learn about Catholicism, I would be lying if I were to say that I didn't share some of their concerns. Before I came to see the Catholic Church as anything other than an evil, man-made institution run by power-hungry men, my understanding of what the Church professed about women could have been boiled down to this: a woman is created to be either a stay-at-home mother with many (many!) children or a stern, legalistic nun with a ruler in hand, looking for a child to slap. Regardless of which path she took, a woman would never be called to leadership, and she was to keep her thoughts to herself, particularly in the presence of men.

Needless to say, I never imagined the Catholic Church as being a place—*the* place—to which every woman was meant to belong and to call home. Of course, I would soon realize that my personal understanding of what it meant to be a woman really wasn't much better than the ideas I attributed to the Church. Over the course of my teenage years, I had internalized the message that being a woman was about being *attractive*. In order to live up to this image of the ideal woman, I thought I had to look beautiful at all times (while appearing blissfully unaware of it and carefree), all the while maintaining an air of mystery around me. This perception of myself led to frequent self-objectification, effectively reducing my own personhood to appearance. I began to resent my body because I often felt that I wasn't attractive enough.

Quite unexpectedly, my conversion to the Church was what would help free me from this tangled web of expectations. Through a long series of events, I eventually started RCIA and was confirmed at age nineteen. I had found a home in the Church: in the unity of her teachings, in the Eucharist, in the sacraments. I had come to see the Catholic Church as the one Body of Christ, the Church Jesus began (see Mt 16:18) centuries ago. Many of the concerns initially raised by my loved ones about the Church's teachings regarding women, however, still remained with me. But, at that point, I knew enough about the Church to see that Catholicism was very different from what I had initially made it out to be. I had also been wrong about many of the Church's teachings before, so I was aware that I might not have the full picture.

Soon enough, I began to make friends with more actual, living, breathing Catholic women. As one might guess, they were very different from what I expected! Some of the women, however, did struggle with me to understand who we were as Catholic women and our place in the Church. Within my particular Catholic cultural context, I was bombarded with talks on dating chastely and the importance of dressing modestly (with little focus on modesty as a virtue that impacts other aspects of life). I heard a strong cultural emphasis on the need for women to submit to men in relationships, with an underemphasis on Saint John Paul II's (and Saint Paul's!) call for men and women to *mutually* submit to each other within marriage.[1] The women's conferences and retreats I attended often revolved around themes such as knowing we're beautiful in God's eyes or discerning a vocation to married or religious life. Though some of this is not necessarily wrong or bad, what was communicated to me was that a woman's purpose in the world is reduced to her looks, her relationship to men, and the function of her biology. This view was remarkably similar to the understanding of womanhood that I knew from growing up in my Evangelical communities. Unfortunately, I heard little focus on a woman's unique ability to lead and to protect human life. And the lives of strong women saints like Joan of Arc or Hildegard were rarely discussed. I felt a disconnect between the actual teachings of the Church and the expectations placed upon women within this particular Catholic cultural context.

The turning point came when I sat down one evening to read Saint John Paul II's *Letter to Women* for the first time. If I could, I would quote the entire letter because it's so liberating. But these passages were the ones that have really helped me distill the Church's understanding of woman from the cultural expectations of women that I had experienced:

On Asking for Forgiveness for Members of Church Who Have Contributed to the Oppression of Women

Women's dignity has often been unacknowledged and their prerogatives misrepresented; they have often been relegated to the margins of society and even reduced to servitude. . . . And if objective blame, especially in particular historical contexts, has belonged to not just a few members of the Church, for this I am truly sorry. May this regret be transformed, on the part of the whole Church, into a renewed commitment of fidelity to the Gospel vision. When it comes to setting women free from every kind of exploitation and domination, the Gospel contains an ever relevant message that goes back to the *attitude of Jesus Christ himself.*

On the Dignity of Women and Their Impact on the World

Women have contributed to [history] as much as men, and more often than not, they did so in much more difficult conditions. . . . To this great, immense feminine "tradition" humanity owes a debt that can never be repaid. Yet how many women have been and continue to be valued more for their physical appearance than for their skill, their professionalism, their intellectual abilities, their deep sensitivity; in a word, the very dignity of their being!

On the Need for Women's Presence in Society and the Church

It is thus my hope, dear sisters, that you will reflect carefully on what it means to speak of the *"genius of women"*, not only in order to be able to see in this phrase a specific part of God's plan which needs to be accepted and appreciated, but also in order to let this genius be more fully expressed in the life of society as a whole, as well as in the life of the Church.[2]

As I read, I started to find clarity. Though it was just a start, I began to realize that the meaning of womanhood is not found in the way a woman looks, or in her docility to any given man, or simply in her ability to birth children.

After finishing *Letter to Women*, I read *Mulieris Dignitatem, On the Dignity and Vocation of Women* (a similar, but longer, and more theologically extensive text from Saint John Paul II); I also began to study Catholic social teaching and learn more about the lives of the saints. All this led me to a series of breakthrough moments like the one I had experienced when I first read *Letter to Women*. I began to understand more fully the richness of the Church's teaching in regard to the meaning of womanhood. Eventually, I felt called to start The Catholic Woman, a multimedia platform dedicated to inspiring millennial Catholic women to find belonging in the Church and to live out their faith by illustrating the many faces and callings of women in the Church, through things like documentaries, interviews, and letters.

Along this journey, the witnesses of saintly women like Mary, the Mother of the Church; Catherine of Siena; Saint Joan of Arc; Saint Hildegard of Bingen; and Saint Teresa Benedicta of the Cross have helped me to discover that embracing femininity is ultimately about cultivating a God-given disposition of openness toward the human person and living it out in whatever way we are called by God. To be a woman is to live a disposition of open attentiveness to the human person in a unique way—a sign of which we can see within our own bodies and therefore express in a uniquely feminine way. If we choose to embrace our feminine disposition, or our "feminine genius" as Saint John Paul II calls it, we can carry it wherever God calls us, whether into marriage, motherhood, the convent, the workplace, or somewhere else.

Womanhood, from the Church's perspective, can't be reduced to a specific set of traits to which each of us must aspire. Many of us feel this way, however. We feel that if we don't live up to the unspoken or spoken expectations around us that there won't be room for us in the Church. But womanhood is about *being*. It's about embracing and accepting who we already are and called to be by God and living that out in light of the Gospel. At the heart of our absolutely essential place in the Church is a call to cultivate belonging within her, to *be* belonging within her, and to invite others to know the love of God within her.

Setting Expectations

In the coming pages, this anthology explores the many different ways we live out our unique attentiveness to the human person as women in the context of the Catholic faith. You'll find personal letters from twenty-five Catholic women, from all sorts of backgrounds, interests, and states in life. You'll hear from mothers, religious sisters, entrepreneurs, artists, activists, and authors. In each letter, the writer will share a personal story that illustrates how she lives out her attentiveness to the human person within her unique identity and call from God. In order to provide a framework that helps illustrate the ways this feminine ethos can unfold and develop, the letters are organized thematically in five sections: receive, create, protect, lead, and nurture.

My hope is that these letters will inspire you to more fully live out your unique call as a woman, wherever God calls you, whether it be in your home, in your community, or in your career. As Saint Teresa Benedicta of the Cross once wrote:

> Only subjective delusion could deny that women are capable of practicing vocations other than that of spouse and mother. . . . [I]ndividual gifts and tendencies can lead to the most diversified activities. Indeed, no woman is *only* woman; like a man, each has her individual specialty and talent, and this talent gives her the capability of doing professional work, be it artistic, scientific, technical, etc. Essentially, the individual talent can enable her to embark on any discipline. . . . The participation of women in the most diverse professional disciplines could be a blessing for the entire society, private or public, precisely if the specifically feminine ethos would be preserved.[3]

Thus, in the coming pages, we'll see twenty-five examples of this feminine ethos lived out in Catholic women's lives today.

Before I conclude, two disclaimers! First, every woman featured in this book could have written a letter for the other four featured sections. For instance, any of the writers truly could have been featured in the "lead" section. I mention this simply because the point of this book is not to box women into different categories nor to indicate that only some women are called to be receptive while others are called to be creative. Rather, the intention is to examine the different characteristics of the feminine ethos and how these characteristics might be carried out amid different circumstances and states in life. That said, it's still helpful to view these women's stories through each category's lens as it illuminates certain aspects of God's movements in their lives. It certainly has helped me to get a sense of the different ways that femininity may be lived out in the context of our great faith.

Second, because each woman is unique, there's a diverse range of stories and viewpoints in the letters ahead. As you read, you'll likely find women to whom you relate with great ease, and others with whom you don't—and that's perfectly okay. When letters feel unfamiliar, I invite you to prayerfully lean in and ask God to reveal his grace to you within that woman's voice and story. All the different letters in this book demonstrate the variety and beauty found among Catholic women and in the Church herself. The diverse chorus of women's voices in the pages ahead echoes something unified, something mysterious and clear about woman herself and also about the Church herself. The Church is both one and universal; in our difference we are called to unity in her. These letters also serve as a testament to how God's grace can be found in any circumstance, including your own.

Finally, dear reader, I pray that this book—through letters, women saints' wisdom, quotes, reflection questions, and prayers—will leave you inspired to reflect on the ways God is calling you to live out your femininity along the path of your own unique vocation. And if you've ever questioned your place in the Church or are not even sure you want to be a part of it anymore, I pray that you will discover in this book a rich, pulsing mosaic of odd-tales, human heartache, vulnerability, sincerity, and joy—pieced together only by God's grace. Listen carefully because as these women pour out their letters, bleeding and beating as one, you might also hear them whisper into your heart, "You belong here too."

Onward and upward,

— *Corynne*

I

Nurture

Providing hospitality for a group of new friends

Buying coffee for a homeless person

Being a supportive presence to a family member in need

In this section, we'll examine how femininity can be expressed through a nurturing presence and showing care for others. In these letters, Catholic women reflect on how they have come to embrace their capacity to nurture and to be attentive to those around them in their own unique ways.

Abby Ellis

Abby describes the sense of belonging she found in the arms of her mother at her family's dinner table and how this experience of belonging helped her return to the Church.

Justina Kopp

Justina shares how becoming a mother of quadruplets and her family heritage have profoundly influenced how she lives the art of nurturing.

Leticia Ochoa Adams

Leticia shares how her son Anthony's suicide has shaped her understanding of what it means to truly love others.

Sister Helena Burns

Sister Helena shares an experience of spiritual motherhood with a young teen that had extraordinary results.

Andrea Polito

Andrea shares how, as a consecrated woman, she cared for a friend who was dying and in doing so discovered the beauty of simply being present.

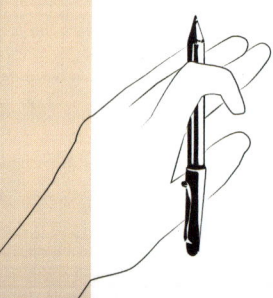

Teresa Benedicta of the Cross

Born in 1891 to a Jewish family in Breslau, Prussia, Edith Stein was a remarkably intelligent and precocious child. She would eventually pursue a doctorate in philosophy, an unusual path for a woman in that time. Though she was a professed atheist since age fourteen, she became interested in Catholicism after reading Saint Teresa of Ávila's autobiography. When she was thirty, Edith was baptized and entered the Church. About a decade later, she entered a Carmelite convent in Cologne, Germany, and took the name Sister Teresa Benedicta of the Cross.

Aware of what was happening to Jewish people in Nazi Germany, Sister Teresa Benedicta felt called to intercede to God on behalf of her people. Like Queen Esther, God called her to plead to her king on behalf of her nation.[4] Just a couple of months after the brutal violence of *Kristallnacht* on November 9, 1938, Sister Teresa Benedicta's prioress had her smuggled across the border to the Netherlands.[5] In a letter to her prioress on Passion Sunday in March of 1939, Sister Teresa Benedicta heroically requested permission to offer her life to Jesus as a sacrifice for true peace.[6]

Just a few years later, her request would be heard. On the morning of August 2, 1942, Sister Teresa Benedicta and her sister Rosa (who had also become Catholic) were arrested by the Gestapo in the convent chapel and taken to Auschwitz. One of the last people to witness Sister Teresa Benedicta at Auschwitz wrote this account of her actions before her death:

> Among the prisoners who were brought in on August 5, Sr. Benedicta stood out on account of her great calmness and composure. The distress in the barracks, and the stir caused by the new arrivals, was indescribable. Sr. Benedicta was just like an angel, going around among the women, comforting them, helping them, and calming them. Many of the mothers were near to distraction; they had not bothered about their children the whole

day long, but just sat brooding in dumb despair. Sr. Benedicta took care of the little children, washed them and combed them, looked after their feeding and their other needs. During the whole of her stay there, she was so busy washing and cleaning as acts of loving kindness that everyone was astonished.[7]

Shortly after, Sister Teresa Benedicta and her sister Rosa were murdered in the gas chambers.

In the darkest of circumstances, Saint Teresa Benedicta of the Cross loved and nurtured those around her. Thus, she is a model of the beauty of the feminine gift of presence to those in need of God's love. In the coming letters, you'll find examples of women who have loved others to the point of suffering, not out of any kind of self-hate but out of a love for themselves, for God, and for others.

PRAYER TO
SAINT TERESA BENEDICTA
OF THE CROSS

Saint Teresa Benedicta of the Cross, you prayed for, served, and nurtured others up to the moment of your death in a concentration camp. Pray that I may live as lovingly and sacrificially as you did.

A Place
at the Table

Dear Sisters,

I met Jesus through my mama at age five. While circling the dining room table, I asked her about heaven. And while placing knives and forks on napkins in preparation for a meal, she spoke of the Cross. She spoke of Jesus. Then she held out her arms, hands clasped in a circle, and invited me in, the way she always did. I ducked under her arms and into her embrace; there I learned about presence and place. In that circle of belonging, I learned my name.

Around the table, my family shared food, story, and time. We lingered for hours with lasagna, black coffee, and laughter, recalling tales of my army-family's travels. Stories of all we'd seen and done. While overseas, my mama hosted cadets, cousins, priests, and friends from around the world. She made a table so inviting that I've lingered next to her there, if only in my mind, for more than thirty-five years.

My family shared space on Sundays too—the six of us hand in hand, thigh to thigh, and kneeling shoulder to shoulder in church pews. While traveling, we celebrated Mass wherever we were able. We partook of the Eucharist in airports, in hotel rooms, and on European trains. We shared Communion in an Israeli kibbutz, down a catacomb in Rome, and at a small side chapel in Saint Peter's. I equated the Mass with family, not location, and Communion with relationship, not just a meal. Wherever we were, we broke bread. Our life was liturgy. We ate together, worshipped together, and as a family on the move, we kept time together. Our table was universal. And deeply intimate.

Today, it feels like my whole life has been wrapped up in my mama, her table, and the Mass. Her favorite places were at home with us and with Jesus in Communion. In my mind her home table and the Church table are inseparable. Sisters, recently I lost my mama. One summer day after my sprawling family had gathered for weeks of togetherness, she quietly went to sleep on her couch. Then she didn't wake up. On the day she died, she had attended Mass in the morning. Then she had served the poor. On her final day, she partook of Jesus in the Eucharist. Then she gave him away.

As far back as I can remember, I had watched my mama cry over the Eucharist. She cried while giving it away, cried while receiving it, cried while thanking God for it, cried while kneeling and missing her own mama. I imagine she cried too when I walked away from the Eucharist for a long season. I often wonder how long she had heaven always on her mind, knowing the Mass is as close as we can get. I wonder if she'd been preparing us our whole lives to be without her, for the moment she would say goodbye. Because how else do you prepare your beloved ones for the heavenly banquet? By teaching them to return, remain, eat, drink, linger, and give thanks long after you've gone. How else but by setting the table again and again. By inviting, serving, nourishing.

On the morning my mama left us, I ran through the dark to her home. After kissing her face, holding her hand, and steadying my father, I ran to the altar at church. Then I ran home. In my disoriented despair, in my mother-hunger, in my search for comfort, I sought out communion. Messy, vulnerable, and confused—I went to Mass. But, you need to know: there was a time when it wasn't so.

By age ten, my scrapbooks bulged with postcards from our family's travels. My souvenirs impressed at show-and-tell, and yet, my favorite places remained home and church—family dinner and the Mass—just like my mama. Still, there came a time when I left my place at the table. In my high-school years, my siblings moved away one after another. Suddenly I stood alone between my parents in the pew at church. Mealtime felt sparse; everyone who had colored the pages of my growing-up years was gone. The places that had named and nourished me became places of scarcity. My tables were turning.

Questions about Catholicism left me confused and defensive. *Why confession, why the saints, why Mary? Is faith alone enough or is Scripture the final authority? What about Martin Luther?* My experiences couldn't withstand pointed questions from critics. My innocent love of family and food couldn't make up for what I lacked in catechesis. Misunderstood in the crowd, I began to choose comfort over confrontation. I stayed silent about my faith. Instead of leaning into the table, I pulled away.

By age eighteen, I had left altogether. I saw my mama's sad eyes as she watched me wander away.

When you leave the family table, you leave a part of yourself behind, for better or worse. For the next several years I forgot how to nourish my body and soul. I settled for cheap fare in places that required little of me. I fed on crumbs, blended in, and mistook sameness for security. When you have no real place, no eyes across the table to meet and mirror your own, no real food for your very real hunger, you begin to wonder if you just might disappear.

After graduating from college, I waited ten more years to return to the Church. Once married, I dove into a vibrant nondenominational community with my new husband. We studied, served, and led. We busied ourselves with great things for God. We gained knowledge and tools for ministry, lived among and led alongside the best of the best. But I felt chronically underfed. Once or twice a year, I would wander in and out of Mass alone, like a hungry stray. Always hiding in the back, I'd kneel as the full weight of my burden rested on my knees, and I would wait for those words: "Happy are those called to the supper of the Lamb." I *was* happy. Mass was the home I longed for and couldn't create. The mealtime I missed. All the while, my mama did what she did best: invited me into her arms, into her home, fed us around her table. She stayed present, tender, and kind. She watched, waited, and prayed.

Later, when my father was ordained to the diaconate, I joined my family for a special Mass. After inhaling the entire hour like fresh air, I leaned into the shoulder of my childhood priest and casually whispered, "We're never really full without Communion are we?" He returned the lean with a smile—a quiet counter-gesture that affirmed and invited. *Whenever you are ready.*

Then, on Holy Thursday, I closed the final chapter of a favorite book that spoke intimately of the Last Supper. There on the page, I read the author's question that I could no longer ignore: "How much communion do you really want to have with me?" The question spilled over my heart and landed in my gut. I sensed that Jesus himself was inviting me home. Soul-hungry and sure, I sped to church before I could overthink. At Mass, during the washing of the feet, my tears fell hard, splashing on the concrete between my shoes. I wiped my nose on my sleeve like a toddler without a tissue. I watched the crowd walk forward for Communion, hands outstretched. And on that evening commemorating the institution of the Eucharist, I watched men and women prostrated in adoration until midnight. I couldn't bear to leave. And I knew I was home.

Christ's call was simple and clear: "Take and eat" (Mt 26:26). "Love . . . as I have loved you" (Jn 15:12, NRSV). It was time. And so I talked to my husband. For months he read book after book while propped up on his pillow in the evening. Then one night, he stated clear as day, "If the Eucharist is real, then how can we stay away?" His certainty trumped every question we could fathom, both socially and theologically. His uncomplicated assurance reminded me of my mama. I remembered her simplicity and quiet trust—how they kept her focused and unencumbered. Fully present, without judgment and criticism. She often spoke of how she wanted to be more knowledgeable, more articulate, and more involved. But it was the simplicity of her faith that made her so beautifully accessible to so many. Sisters, Jesus' gift of the Eucharist is not meant to be complicated or cumbersome. That night, I laid my burden down. My husband and I acknowledged our common hunger. Then we brought our family back to the Table.

Sisters, we have to know where our home is. Where our *meal* is. We have to know how to gather and stay, feed one another good food, and fill up on togetherness and time and touch. This is how we will change the world. Around the table. Inside our homes. Receiving love and giving it away. My mama did it again and again. And now? I see and remember her everywhere: in every story, every song, every kind and tender moment. Every phone call, every morning cup of coffee, every flower, every birdsong. Every moment of childlike play. And in every Mass. There she is, present to me. That was always her way. And sisters, you need to know: it's Jesus' way. Even more than our loved ones in the communion of saints, Jesus is with us all the time. In every nook and cranny of our lives and all our comings and goings—he is there. Inescapable. Ready. Full of beauty, goodness, and truth. Grace and comfort. He's calling your name, delighting in you, and dying to nourish you.

The night before my mama's funeral, hundreds came to keep watch and pray. In a vulnerable moment, I put my head on a sister's shoulder and whisper-cried, "Is it crazy that I'm excited for the Eucharist tomorrow? I can't wait to gather around the table with my mama one more time." The next day, we celebrated the Mass, and we celebrated my mama's life. We ate and pondered heaven, and we were filled. And then we commended her to the angels on the prayers of fragrant incense that rose toward heaven. My mama was the sweet scent of Christ. I believe that to have known her was to have seen Jesus. And now, I believe she is happy. Because *happy are those called to the supper of the Lamb.*

Today, my family of eight is at home in the Catholic Church. Our lives and hearts are full. Each night we sit around the table. We laugh, cry, and connect. I watch for hunger cues, and I remember how my mama fed us well, with intention and kindness. At the table, we relish the good moments and reconcile the bad—always repairing, always remembering that we are but dust (see Ps 103:14). We stay until the meal is finished, until our hearts and bellies are full. We stay because it was always the staying that was the best part. The lingering, the presence, and the being seen. This is the place I was named. This is the place I learned of heaven. This is the place that called me home. And this is the place where we will meet again.

Being nourished well around my mama's table, falling in love with the Eucharist beside her, and even losing her has reminded me, forevermore, that I belong at the table. Sisters, you were made to be named, nurtured, and nourished at the family table too. Perhaps your table did not look much like mine. Sisters, people can and have done great harm. But there's a meal that won't leave you hungry or hurt. You are invited to stay and be seen. Stay until you know your name and your place. It's okay if it takes a while. He's after your heart. Stay until you're filled. And then? Go home and set a table. Go out and fill others.

Just as my mama ate a sacred meal and then served meals to many more, we too are called to be nourished by Communion, so that we might go out again and nourish. And someday, when we leave this earth, we'll leave behind beloved ones who know their place, what to consume, and what to give away. Hearts that know their names—and Jesus' name too. Hearts that love to linger at the Table. And you, Sister? Your soul will rise on the prayers of fragrant incense as your loved ones announce together, "Surely, *she* was the aroma of Christ. The Mass is ended. Now go! Let us become what we've received."

Sisters, a meal is prepared and your place is waiting.

Come to the table.

Most sincerely,

Abby Ellis

Sisters, people can and have done great harm. But there's a meal that won't leave you hungry or hurt. You are invited to stay and be seen: Stay until you know your name and your place. It's ok if it takes a while. He's after your heart. ♥ Stay until you're filled. And then? Go home and set a table. Go out and fill others. A heart that has been fed can't help but overflow.

ABBY ELLIS is a wife of eighteen years and a mama to six. She teaches her children, ages four to fourteen, in her home on the East Coast. A nurse by trade, she is currently training to care for those who find themselves in wounded places, where the hope of the Gospel collides with stories of trauma and harm. A writer at heart, she scribbles down words to help her see. Abby loves beauty, story, humanity, and the Church. She believes in a wild, tender Father who pursues; and she holds out audacious hope for Christian unity around one table.

Reflection Question and Prayer

"But there's a meal that won't leave you hungry or hurt. Please don't leave the table. Please stay and be seen. Stay until you know your name and your place. It's okay if it takes a while. He's after your heart. Stay until you're filled. And then? Go out and fill others. Go home and set a table. Tell others where you found your sustenance."

Take a moment to meditate on the Eucharist and how Christ has been true nourishment for you. Reflect on the ways you are living a Eucharistic life. How could you better bring the nourishment found in the Mass to those around you?

Pray a Hail Mary for growth in a Eucharistic spirituality and for those who have fallen away from the Church. May they rediscover the love of God in the sacraments in a new and radical way. Then, close with this section's petition:

Saint Teresa Benedicta of the Cross, you prayed for, served, and nurtured others up to the moment of your death in a concentration camp. Pray that I may live as lovingly and sacrificially as you did.

My Body, Given Up for You

Dear Sisters,

Hello from southwestern Kenya! If you were to drive through the winding Kisii Highlands, one of the most striking things you would notice is the lush, green landscape. Verdant hills seem to stretch on forever, dotted with the shiny metal rooftops of homes built on small plots of land. As you drive the winding roads, you would easily recognize the nurturing happening here. You would see families tending their crops in their small *shambas* (farms). You would observe mothers carrying babies, wrapped in brightly colored *kitambaas* (fabric), on their backs. Once, I spotted a mama taking a rest in the grass as she breastfed her fussing baby. Both great tenderness and strength can be seen in that life, in that work. I've been to Kenya ten times, and while each trip is so different, this is my first time here as a mother. The image of those hardworking women really stays with me.

When people find out that my husband, Matthew, and I have quadruplets, one of the first questions they usually ask is, "How did you react when you found out there were four?" For pretty obvious reasons, forever etched in my memory is the day we learned of the tiny, but mighty, party happening in my uterus. Because my first pregnancy ended in an early miscarriage, when I went for a sonogram, my anxiety was through the roof. I was convinced that my pregnancy would end just as the first did. I didn't trust my body to nurture and to protect the life within me. So imagine my surprise when there was not one, but *four* gestational sacs on the screen. As the sonographer cheerfully labeled the babies A, B, C, and D, my husband and I did the only thing one can do when your family explodes from two to six: laugh! We laughed for two solid days because it was truly hilarious. Mind you, we had been married for about five minutes (okay, more like seven months) at this point. It was pure joy.

After those two days, we started to panic about logistics. We googled and read way more things than we should have, and the reality began to set in. No matter what, though, we would love these four babies, just like their sibling who came before them. They were also tiny and fragile with an increased risk of miscarriage, so I also was terrified. I wanted to do whatever I could to hold onto these babies. At our first appointment with a perinatologist, we had to defend the life and dignity of each of our kids. The doctor offered us so-called selective reduction (in this case, aborting two babies) as an option, but that was not an option for us. We chose four from the moment we knew there were four.

Did you know that a "quad mom" needs to consume around 4,500 calories and 250 grams of protein per day? For some context, I'm five feet tall and hover around 100 pounds, so eating became my full-time job. And it helped because it felt like something I could control. I ate not only for myself, but also for my growing brood. I took great pride in their growth from week to week at each ultrasound.

During my pregnancy, the Mass and the Eucharist began to take on a richer meaning. Mass was pretty uncomfortable, so I often had to sit and drink water to avoid passing out. The words of the consecration, "This is my Body, given up for you," came alive for me. I couldn't help but weep every time I heard them. All the aches, pains, discomforts, and changes I was experiencing in my body were all for my kids. And I readily accepted all of it out of a love I had never felt before. Of course, my small sacrifice of love is nothing compared to Jesus' sacrifice of love, but something finally clicked for me. This deep love guided me as I walked into the operating room thirty-three weeks pregnant on a beautiful October Sunday morning. Due to preeclampsia, I was unable to remain awake during the C-section and only met my babies after surgery, when they were two hours old. As difficult and even traumatic as that was, it was worth it to keep them healthy and safe.

On the feast of Saint Gerard Majella, patron saint of expectant mothers, I gave birth to itty-bitty quadruplets, a girl and three boys: Cora, Raphael, Theodore, and Benedict. They are the purest little lights of my life. Before my children's birth, when I imagined my life as a mother, I naively thought that I would have my babies one (*maybe* two) at a time, responsibly spaced, with perhaps one Natural Family Planning "surprise" baby sprinkled in there. I imagined the ordinary struggles of motherhood, but I also pictured tender bonding moments, nurturing each of my babies in sacred one-on-one time. The reality now is that my struggles and joys are multiplied! I had envisioned one baby cooing and smiling at me, instead I got a chorus of giggles.

This life is so beautiful and so hard. From the start, I worried about giving each of my tiny babies what they needed and honestly deserved. My insecurity and anxiety only grew after they were born—I cried on the way home from the hospital because I felt I already had not given equal time to each baby. "How will I ever be able to do this once they're home?" I wondered. Yet, just as the struggles and joys were multiplied in this journey of motherhood, so too were the lessons I've learned.

From the moment I knew about our babies, I was very aware that I definitely was not in control. God is. Once my husband went back to work, I also felt inadequate in the face of all that needed to be done. I mean, do the math—four crying babies, two arms, two breasts, one me. There was no way I could ever be enough. This was so different than the motherhood I had dreamed of for myself. I had to let go of that dream and make room for what was in front of me, all I had been given. Matthew and I came up with ways to feed our children simultaneously and keep them on the same schedule. We leaned heavily on our village; between our families and postpartum doulas, we tried to maximize happiness and sleep in our home.

Fast forward to now. The kids are nearly three years old, and we just took them on their first international trip to Kenya, the country my mom is from. You might now be wondering, "You brought four toddlers on an international trip. Are you nuts?" Why yes, yes, we are. Thankfully, my husband is even more adventurous than I am, so he was up to the challenge. This land has always been sacred to my family. It's my maternal ancestral home. It's where my parents, against all odds, met and married. I've always dreamed of passing this place on to my children and having them love it just as my siblings and I do.

Over the years, Kenya has shown me what it means to nurture. The land on which my family's home sits has been in the family for generations. Most of my mom's ten siblings live and raise their children there. My cousins get to grow up right alongside each other, and my aunts all share the responsibilities of keeping up their homes. Together they cook, maintain the compound, and tend to the children. My grandma, a straight-up matriarchal powerhouse who hardly looks like an octogenarian, also shares in the tasks of daily life. (More often than not, though, I catch her smiling with a cooing baby on her lap.)

In my mother's home, it's hard to miss the value of a multigenerational village. There I learned that to nurture means to invest, to cultivate, to draw out, and to raise up each person's worth and dignity with great care and love. I cannot count the number of times in my own mothering that I have reflected particularly on the examples of the Kenyan women in my family. They endure a great deal and have overcome even more. They are fiercely strong and deeply tender, so much like our Blessed Mother, Mary. Like her, their lives are not easy, yet they face great trials with great love. Now, as a mother reflecting on a lifetime of summer trips to this village, I recognize just how much these women have influenced my definition of nurturing. I am grateful for the strong women in my family who have shown me just how capable and impressive women are. They showed me that a woman's vocation to motherhood was never meant to be easy, but there is nevertheless a striking beauty to bringing children into the world and nurturing them.

As I watch my children playing with their cousins, transcending language barriers with games and laughter the way only children can, my eyes well with tears of joy and pride. Getting to this point, not just by embarking on a cross-continental trip, but beginning on that April day when I learned of my children's very existence, has been no small feat. Such joyful exhaustion, sisters! I never want to let my children's "fourness" prohibit me from giving them a full and beautiful life. It means the world to have my children here in Kenya; this trip means so much more than my kids having the chance to see their favorite animals in the wild. The children are being immersed in a culture rooted in the art of nurturing. It feels deeply good to be here. I never expected motherhood to look like this—but thank God it does.

Saint Gianna Beretta Molla once wrote, "Love and sacrifice are as intimately connected as sun and light. We cannot love without suffering or suffer without loving."[11] This is the heart of a woman. We stretch and break ourselves for others—for love of them and for love of God. So, surround yourself with women and saints who model virtuous nurturing. Cultivate that ability within you and ask Our Lady to show you how you are called to be a nurturer in your life, no matter your vocation or current life state. There is great power in a woman's gentleness and tenderness. Believe in your power.

Love,

Justina Kopp

There is great power in a
woman's gentleness and tenderness.
Believe in your power.

— Justina Kopp

JUSTINA KOPP is a stay-at-home mom who lives in the Twin Cities, Minnesota, with her husband, Matthew, and their quadruplet toddlers: Cora, Raphael, Theodore, and Benedict. She is a graduate of the University of St. Thomas (Minnesota) where she studied Catholic Studies and biology, and she currently serves on the Advisory Board for the Center for Catholic Studies. Before marriage and family life, Justina served as a campus minister at the University of Minnesota's Newman Center. Her life story, marked with the tragic loss of her father in the I-35W bridge collapse and the surprise of her quadruplets, has been told through various media outlets and podcasts. When she's not chasing her kids around, you can find Justina cruising around town with Starbucks in hand, listening to her favorite true-crime podcasts.

Reflection Question and Prayer

"In my mother's home, it's hard to miss the value of a multigenerational village. There I learned that to nurture means to invest, to cultivate, to draw out, and to raise up each person's worth and dignity with great care and love. I cannot count the number of times in my own mothering that I have reflected particularly on the examples of the Kenyan women in my family. They endure a great deal and have overcome even more. They are fiercely strong and deeply tender, so much like our Blessed Mother, Mary."

Which women in your life have shown you the strength of womanhood? Reflect on how you live differently as a result of their presence in your life.

Pray a Hail Mary for the women in your life who have inspired you and for all new mothers. Then, close with this section's petition:

Saint Teresa Benedicta of the Cross, you prayed for, served, and nurtured others up to the moment of your death in a concentration camp. Pray that I may live as lovingly and sacrificially as you did.

"Can a mother forget her infant, be without tenderness for the child of her womb? Even should she forget, I will never forget you."

—Isaiah 49:15

"We cannot love God unless we love each other, and to love we must know each other. We know Him in the breaking of bread, and we know each other in the breaking of bread, and we are not alone anymore. Heaven is a banquet and life is a banquet, too, even with a crust, where there is companionship."[10]

—Dorothy Day

Surrendering Control and Learning to Love

Dear Sister,

My name is Leticia Ochoa Adams, and in March of 2017 my oldest son, Anthony, took his own life in my home. What I have learned from that moment has changed every aspect of my life. I would like to share some of what I have learned with you. On the day my oldest son died by suicide, I was in the middle of a lot of chaos. Bills needed to be paid or the lights were going to be turned off the next day. My two sons in high school were both set to graduate in a couple of months. My daughter was struggling with her gender and sexual orientation. (Or, to be honest, I was the one struggling—she was just figuring out her life in a different time period from when I was a teen.) Also, my husband and I had been having difficulties in our marriage for a long time. And, to top everything off, my oldest son, Anthony, was suffering from mental illness, and we were all at a loss as to how to help him. None of us ever thought that he would take his own life. Even in the moments when I feared the worst, I didn't ever really consider the possibility of suicide.

I definitely did not think I could ever survive losing him.

On March 8, 2017, at 4:45 p.m., before heading out of the house to a meeting, my husband walked into the garage to turn the light off. Instead he found my son's body. At that moment our lives changed forever. Everything I thought I knew about myself, my family, my faith, and my motherhood changed. From the moment my husband found Anthony dead in the garage, my motherly instincts kicked into gear. I knew that my job was to be strong for my other kids, to be their mother, and to be Anthony's mother. But what did that mean? I had never really thought deeply about motherhood before.

When I became pregnant with Anthony, I was just sixteen years old. I went to the hospital forty weeks later, gave birth to a tiny human, and the doctor handed him to me to take care of for the next eighteen years. That's all I knew about motherhood. It's how all the women in my family did motherhood. We took care of our kids, worked hard, and made sure they had everything they needed. It was my job to make sure they had food, clothes, an education, and to make sure they knew how to say "Yes, ma'am" and "Yes, sir" when replying to an adult. But Anthony's suicide blew up the question of motherhood in my life.

In the years and months since that day, I have learned that being a wife and mother means loving in the face of shame, trauma, arrogance, and the damage that comes from mistakes made freely. Before Anthony died, I expected my children to be walking billboards of my worthiness and holiness. I needed them to act a certain way to prove that I was good enough and that I was a good Catholic. I did not want children who made mistakes while trying to figure out life because that would mean that I was somehow failing. A lot of my fear came from being a teen mom who was often told that I would never be able to raise successful human beings. My entire concept of motherhood up until Anthony's death was that mothers were responsible for everything their children do. Because of this, my first thought when I saw Anthony's lifeless body was, "How am I ever going to be able to face anyone again?"

In the process of healing from the loss of Anthony's beautiful life, I have learned that my children have the right to make their own mistakes. And not just my children but my husband too. There are just some things that are between the people I love and God. Things that are none of my business. The only choice I had was to hand it over to God and to pray. I no longer had any other option. I couldn't nag, beg, or guilt Anthony into going to Mass or confession. I couldn't even argue with him that God exists. In the aftermath of my son's suicide, all I could do was to pray for his soul and hope that he had accepted the gift of salvation.

I realized after Anthony's death that I had tricked myself into thinking that I was in control. That was the root of so many of my problems. Since I had become a mother, I thought I could control *everything* so that my children would be safe. Part of that mentality is just what mothers and fathers have to do to survive raising children. But a huge part of our children's lives are out of our control. I have come to realize that more than even safety, I owe my children love and compassion. I cannot even control how my children respond to the offer of salvation—it's between them and God. So what is my role? As their mother, I had my children baptized and tried to raise them in the faith. Now it's my duty as the mother of adult children to love them, to

"Like newborn infants, long for pure spiritual milk so that through it you may grow into salvation, for you have tasted that the Lord is good."

—1 Peter 2:2–3

love God, and to pray. I just try to be an example of someone who is in relationship with God, and I try to accept that my children will do things differently from what I would like (frequently). But I also refuse to give up on the power of God to break through their deafness.

I instilled in my children a love for finding the truth in all things, that I trust will eventually lead them to the Truth himself. Now, whether my children accept the gift of salvation is between God and each of my kids. From there, I've realized that the same goes for my husband, and everyone else. I've stopped thinking it's my job to convince them that God exists and that he loves them more than they think he does. My job is to love people and to be a witness to a life tethered to God's grace. Because honestly, God's grace is the only way I have survived my son's suicide. Without the love of God, I would not be writing this letter right now; I would be lying in the ground next to Anthony. And *that* truth is what I want to tell anyone who will listen.

For those who do not want to hear about God, my job is to love them, to listen to their stories, and to do the very best I can to accept the fact that I am not their savior—Jesus is. One thing I know for sure about Jesus is that he is merciful, and when a person turns to him, he is ready to receive them with open arms, no matter what mistakes a person has made. He did this for me. And other people showed me this kind of love and helped me to encounter the love of God in a real way.

My life has become a lot simpler since I have let go of the fear of looking like a bad Catholic and the false idea that it's somehow my job to save people (that was rooted in pride). Now, I show up where God sends me and I listen to people. Especially my children. I try to listen to them when they share an opinion I disagree with, and I try to remember that this is part of growing up and learning. For instance, each of my children has different political leanings, all of which I disagree with. But I listen to them without correcting them. And when it's my turn to speak, I offer my opinion apart from disagreeing with them. I also ask a lot of questions. I have nothing to prove, and this has opened me up to the gift of new people with new experiences and new stories to share with me. That's the beauty of life. In the shadow of my son's death, I choose to live.

When I feared what people would think of my kids who thought this or that or identified as gay or atheist, none of it came from my love for them as people. In the months since losing Anthony and letting go of my concern for what people thought of my kids, I have seen my surviving children become great human beings. They care for those less fortunate, they volunteer, they seek truth, and they make it a point to honor Anthony's memory with their lives. I had wanted perfect Catholic kids to prove that I was a good Catholic mother, not for the sake of my kids or even for the glory of God. I had simply wanted to prove that I was better than other mothers. All of my fear had stemmed from a fear of not being good enough, and the way I had tried to prove that I was good enough was by judging others.

We are called to love others in the way God loves us. And God loves us no matter what we have done or have not done—but he calls us to be holy. Not because he wants us to earn his love but because he created us to be holy. We are called to love others in the same way. We love people as they are but also in hope for what they can be, and with healthy expectations around what loving us back looks like and does not look like. We cannot force anyone to do anything the way we want. All we can do is to love them and accept them as they are, with boundaries to protect ourselves. Setting boundaries is not about trying to control others but about determining what is and is not a loving way to treat others and for them to treat us. By learning when it's necessary to say "no" to others, we give ourselves room to say "yes" to God.

The true power of womanhood lies in the way we say "yes" to God. Mary's power came through her *fiat*. Before Anthony's death, I had received messages both inside and outside of the Church that gave me a very distorted view of womanhood. From outside the Church, I was told by some that strong women have a good job and a successful career. From inside the Church, I was told by others to not be pushy, show too much skin, or rock the boat. But now that I am the mother of a dead child, I see that my feminine power lies in saying "yes" to God even in the midst of my grief and brokenness. By speaking about Anthony and writing and sharing about my life, I say yes to what God has asked of me and that's where I can be my best self.

I now see that womanhood is powerful, and motherhood is strength and dignity. There's a reason we revere Mary the way we do. It takes strength and dignity to carry human beings in our bodies, birth them, raise them, and then sometimes bury them. To survive taking care of the dead body of a child to whom I had given birth, I had to surrender everything to God. Nothing took as much strength from me as that surrender. In that surrender, I have learned how to love Anthony just as he was and is—I have had no other choice. I cannot do anything else for him other than pray for him and seek healing in order to be the mother he needed me to be when he was alive. I must now accept Anthony as he is because the illusion of controlling him was taken away from me the day he died. And the gift that has come from that is that I have come to love and accept my other children and everyone else in my life in the same way.

In Christ,

Leticia Ochoa Adams

LETICIA OCHOA ADAMS is a convert to Catholicism, a writer, and a speaker. She lost her son Anthony to suicide in 2017, and ever since, she has been on a mission to tell his story to anyone who will listen. Leticia lives in Texas with her husband, her three surviving children, Anthony's two daughters, and three pit bulls. She is also a student at Holy Apostles College and Seminary and is hoping to graduate with a bachelor's degree in philosophy. Through her journey into the Catholic Church and surviving the suicide of her son, Leticia has learned more about herself as a Hispanic woman, wife, and mother—and the strength through God's grace that comes with each of those titles.

From outside the church, I was told
by some, that strong women have
a good job and successful career.
From inside the church, I was told by
others to not be pushy, show too much
skin, or rock the boat. But now what
I am the mother of a dead child,
I see what my feminie power lies
in saying "yes" to God even in the
midst of grief & brokenness

Luticia Ochoa Adams

Reflection Question and Prayer

"My life has become a lot simpler since I have let go of the fear of looking like a bad Catholic and the false idea that it's somehow my job to save people (that was rooted in pride). Now, I show up where God sends me, and I listen to people."

Have you ever let the fear of looking like a "bad Catholic" get in the way of loving someone? Reflect on a time when personal pride has prevented you from loving someone else as God does.

Pray a Hail Mary for a person you have not loved as you should have. Ask the Lord to empower you in the Holy Spirit to love as freely as Christ in the future. Say an additional prayer for those who have been impacted by suicide: for families, communities, and the deceased. Then, close with this section's petition:

Saint Teresa Benedicta of the Cross, you prayed for, served, and nurtured others up to the moment of your death in a concentration camp. Pray that I may live as lovingly and sacrificially as you did.

Spiritual Motherhood Empowers

"Do to all the charity of the Truth."
—Blessed James Alberione, SSP

Dear Friends,

I'm a religious sister of the Daughters of Saint Paul, a congregation founded to use the media to evangelize. When I was a teenager, I was a radical feminist in that I believed that men and women were pretty much identical. I had adopted a one-size-fits-all, generic paradigm for all humans (I would later realize that when one picks a paradigm through which to view all humans, it's generally a masculine one that obliterates the feminine). I didn't hold motherhood in very high esteem, let alone spiritual motherhood. After joining the convent, I read John Paul II's *Theology of the Body,* and it opened my eyes, changed my life, and gave me permission to be a woman. But it's been an ongoing conversion to this way of thinking about men and women, and I learn every day something new about what it means to be a woman.

One frigid Canadian night, I had finished giving a presentation to several youth groups that had come together for the night in a parish center. After the talk, one of the teens approached me (I'll call him Kyle), and he inquired if he could ask me a question. He was a smart, scientifically-minded young person, one of those "atheists" who still goes to youth group. He also was extremely intense and tense; his whole body was like a wound-up spring. Of course, I'm used to young people approaching me after my talks. They ask me additional questions, want something clarified, share an insight, don't agree, want some advice, or simply want to share their stories with me. But that night Kyle's one question turned out to be more like fifty.

Each time Kyle asked me a question, he'd soon realize I had an answer, so instead of listening to my response, he'd cut me off and go on—rapid fire—to the next question. He asked about God, belief, eternity, heaven, hell, free will, evolution, conception, Creation, the universe, the problem of evil—you know, the biggies, the perennial questions that stump us all. Since my youth, though, I've been asking all these same questions so I have found simple, clear, and convincing ways to respond to them. He wasn't asking me anything new or anything for which I didn't have a prefab answer. Dissatisfied that his questions hadn't yet led to a "gotcha" moment, Kyle's Inquisition dragged on. Meanwhile, other young people from his youth group kept coming over to us and pleading, "Kyle! We have to go!" They were understandably restless; they had driven from God-knows-where in the freezing cold, dead-of-winter, and they were ready to go home. Their youth ministers, however, didn't seem eager to leave. Instead they were observing us from time to time. I could read on their faces that they wanted Kyle to talk to me. I resolved that when the first youth minister said it was time to go, I would end our conversation.

As I was being pummeled with queries, I observed that Kyle was sincere and thoughtful; he really wanted answers. So I prayed, "O God, please let me see what's really going on here. Let me know what's really on his heart. Let it be revealed and let me be able to help him." I knew that many people make an intellectual journey to the Lord and to faith. We are, however, not just brains in vats; we each have our own emotional journey, our whole-person journey to God: mind, will, and heart. And our experiences and wounds sometimes can provide intellectual stumbling blocks that need healing and clearing away. Many obstacles that seem like clear-cut disagreements of reason and facts can actually be matters of the heart. As Blaise Pascal once wrote, "The heart has its reasons, which reason does not know."[12]

Suddenly (if there can be a "suddenly" after one hour of relentless questioning), Kyle asked me, "Can I ask you about one more thing?" Then he shared with me the hurt that had been on his heart the whole time. It had shaped his vision of himself and his worth as a person: Kyle had been told by his father that he had been an "accident."

The profound pain of rejection in those words caused Kyle to physically hang his head as he spoke; it was as though a heavy burden were crushing him. Because I knew time was of the essence (the youth group was still waiting after all), I swiftly responded to this false, abominable lie, proclaiming unequivocally, "Kyle. You're not an accident. Your parents had sex." For the first time, Kyle broke out into a broad smile, and some tension evaporated. I continued, "There's no such thing as an accident baby or an oops baby or a surprise baby or a mistake baby. Sex equals babies. Kyle, it's sad if our parents don't want us, at least at first. But ultimately, it doesn't matter because God wants us. The fact that you're standing here today means that God wanted you. God is our Creator. God is our good Father. Even if we don't have a good father here on earth, God is a good Father, and he's everything and more than we could ever want in our own fathers." More tension evaporated. Then I spoke a bit to Kyle about forgiveness and the importance of praying for his dad. By this time, Kyle was crying, I was crying, and I got not one but two hugs. The burden on his heart had lifted, and he was now ready to go.

Though this encounter took place years ago, it has stayed on my heart ever since. The Lord was present to Kyle in his need that evening, and he was also present to me, revealing to me an aspect of my vocation I had perhaps not seen so clearly before. This sad but beautiful experience affirmed many things for me as a Catholic woman and a religious sister. First, I just love young people. They're halfway between childhood and adulthood and still have the innocence and passion of youth but also some of the sophistication and burdens of maturity. And, honestly, today's youth are facing challenges that no other generation has ever had to face. Many are neglected through a lack of parenting. They experience practical atheism all around them. Most are allowed an unbridled use of media devices. Kids are sexualized at younger and younger ages, and false gender ideology makes them doubt their identities and the nature of reality at the most fundamental levels. All this makes me angry and want to fight for them. Sometimes we think we should misrepresent or water down the faith for them, but we should never do that for them or for anyone! Even when people can't initially accept the truth, only the truth will save.

This experience also confirmed for me the reality of spiritual motherhood. What is spiritual motherhood? Whenever a living organism matures, it gives life, bears fruit, and gives back. Every man is a spiritual father because whenever he loves, helps, does charity, he does it *as* a man, as a spiritual father. Every woman is a spiritual mother because whenever she loves, helps, does charity, she does it *as* a woman, as a spiritual mother. As a spiritual mother by vocation, I have the time, ability (and duty!) to spend an hour with a hurting teen.

Finally, this experience confirmed my mission as a Daughter of Saint Paul to practice the often unknown and undervalued Spiritual Works of Mercy: instruct the ignorant, counsel the doubtful, admonish the sinner, comfort the sorrowful, forgive injuries, bear wrongs patiently, and pray for the living and the dead. My favorite of these is the first, "instruct the ignorant." The devil has convinced our age that knowledge and wisdom are unimportant. "Just feel and do," we're told over and over. But how do we interpret and deal with our feelings? What are we supposed to do (and not do), and how do we do it?

Everyone, even people who are not intellectually inclined, need something for their minds to chew on. Our minds are meant to direct us. The mind is "queen" and needs to direct our wills and hearts. Blessed James Alberione, the founder of the Daughters of Saint Paul, wrote an entire book, *Sanctification of the Mind*, on the importance of the mind. But life is not just a head trip; we need healing for our wills and our hearts as well. And I believe that some simple knowledge of the truth was healing for Kyle: "My people are ruined for lack of knowledge!" (Hos 4:6).

All women, including you, have the capacity to be spiritual mothers. So be confident in your womanhood, and reach out with your feminine gifts, your own unique way of thinking, loving, and problem solving. By embracing your spiritual motherhood, you empower our young people to embrace their identity as beloved men and women of God.

Sincerely in Jesus and Mary,

Sister Helena Raphael

All women, including you, have the capacity to be spiritual Mothers. So be confident in your womanhood and reach out with your feminine gifts, your own unique way of thinking, loving, and problem solving. By embracing your spiritual Motherhood, you empower our young people to embrace their identity as beloved men and women of God.

Sr. Helena Raphael, FSP

Sister Helena Raphael Burns, FSP, has a master's in media literacy education and studied screenwriting at UCLA. She also holds a certificate in pastoral youth ministry and studied at the Theology of the Body Institute in Pennsylvania. She gives media literacy and Theology of the Body workshops to youth and adults all over Canada and the United States. She reviews movies for The Catholic Channel on SiriusXM. She wrote and directed a documentary that can be found at tinyurl.com/AlberioneFilm. Her hobbies include bird watching, chess, coffee, and hockey. You can find her on Twitter @SrHelenaBurns and Instagram @SisterHelenaBurns.

Reflection Question and Prayer

"All women, including you, have the capacity to be spiritual mothers. So be confident in your womanhood, and reach out with your feminine gifts, your own unique way of thinking, loving, and problem solving. By embracing your spiritual motherhood, you empower our young people to embrace their identity as beloved men and women of God."

Take some time to think of the young people around you. When you're with them, do you listen to them and try to understand their stories, hopes, and concerns? How can you step more into your spiritual motherhood in order to empower others?

Say a Hail Mary for young people, that they may be served well by the faithful and find a home in the Church. Then, close with this section's petition:

Saint Teresa Benedicta of the Cross, you prayed for, served, and nurtured others up to the moment of your death in a concentration camp. Pray that I may live as lovingly and sacrificially as you did.

"Woman's intrinsic value can work in every place and thereby institute grace. . . . Everywhere she meets with a human being, she will find opportunity to sustain, to counsel, to help."[9]

—Edith Stein

"Whether she is a mother in the home or occupies a place in the limelight of public life or lives behind her cloister walls, [a woman] must be the handmaid of the Lord everywhere. So had the Mother of God in all circumstances of her life. . . . Were each woman an image of the Mother of God, a Spouse of Christ, an apostle of the Divine Heart, then would each fulfill her feminine vocation no matter what conditions she lived in and what worldly activity absorbed her."[8]

—Saint Edith Stein

Being Not Doing

My Sister,

If there were a club for melodramatic, inappropriate, overly emotional, insecure Italian women, I would certainly be the president. So you can imagine my surprise when the Lord called me to the vocation of consecrated virginity. I was always one of those people who assumed that those who gave their lives to the Church would always have it together. Priests, nuns, monks, consecrated people—they always seemed to be at a different level of peace, joy, love (and all the other good things we hear so much just about). Clearly, the owl delivering the message inviting me to the heavenly Hogwarts was thrown *way* off course.

But the Lord knew what he was doing, and the means by which I heard his call was through Saint Mary Magdalene. Stories all over the Gospels traditionally associated with Mary Magdalene paint a picture of a woman who needed Jesus: to cast out her demons, to forgive her, to heal her, to receive him in her home. She too seemed "unfit" for the life to which the Lord called her. Her story was one of conversion, over and over and over again. This "unfit" woman seemed a very fitting guide as I discerned my vocation; I followed her to Jesus.

By a miracle of grace, a few years ago I was consecrated to a life of perpetual virginity on July 22, Saint Mary Magdalene's feast day. As the months following my consecration progressed, nothing was as I had anticipated. Relationships fell apart, misunderstandings grew, and I was constantly asking myself what I should have done differently. I kept returning to my patroness, asking for her wisdom and guidance. The Lord kept bringing me back to one question, "What did Mary Magdalene do that was so special?" The only answer I ever came up with was that she simply watched and prayed (see Mt 26:41).

When I first started discerning a call to consecrated virginity, I embarked on a five-year journey of study and prayer. I learned about three aspects of this vocation—virgin, spouse, and mother. "Virgin" I understood. A commitment to perpetual virginity for the sake of the kingdom of God allows for a radical availability to God's work. "Spouse" also made sense. Radical availability allows for a deeper spousal intimacy with Christ. "Mother," however, seemed trickier to me. Spiritual motherhood is the source of fruitfulness for the consecrated virgin. But I wondered, "Lord, how do I live this?" The only person I could think of as an example was Our Lady, and how could I even begin to learn from the perfect woman? I always knew I would have been a good mother, but the thought of even praying about spiritual motherhood was intimidating. So I did what any self-respecting, overly emotional Italian woman would do: I cried and ignored the issue. In my depths, I knew that the Lord would reveal himself to me on this subject, but I didn't go seeking answers.

Consecrated virginity is lived in the world, so I continued to work and live as I had before. I am a pediatric, oncology nurse who works with children suffering from cancer. I've been doing this work for over a decade. That means, unfortunately, I have become very well-acquainted with death. I hold fast to the possibility of a good and holy death for anyone and have accompanied many patients and their families in this process for many years. But, as anyone who has experienced the death of a loved one knows, death is completely different when it becomes personal.

Days before my thirtieth birthday, my spiritual grandfather, a priest and dear friend, was diagnosed with stage four esophageal cancer. Due to how he was feeling and his experience watching other loved ones fight cancer, he decided to forego treatment and spend his final days preparing to be with Christ. He called me to ask for advice, insight, and about what he should expect. He also had one simple request, "Andréa, I don't want to die alone." I don't think I will ever understand why my friend asked this of me or why the Lord called me to accompany him in death. Perhaps because I'm a nurse, perhaps because I'm consecrated, perhaps because I was one of the few people he felt he could entrust with this task. It was the Lord's work— that's all I know.

On the fortieth day of my friend's suffering, I was alone at his bedside, watching him struggle to breathe. My instincts were very concrete. I counted the seconds between his breaths as they grew farther and farther apart. I moved him from side to side to try to alleviate the rattle in his chest. All day long I attempted to ease his suffering in some way, and it was all for naught. Nothing changed. He was dying, and all I could do was watch. I spent many hours that day trying to figure out what more I could do and trying to understand why this was happening. I felt so helpless.

As I sat there helpless, I reflected on my own mother and how she loved me. Even when I was a depressed, angsty teenager who could not see past the pain of the current minute, pain I thought was earth-shattering and life-limiting. I had no hope and was a stubborn teenager, a terrible combination. During that time, my mom suffered my behavior in silence in a way that I will never understand fully. She wept over me, and she prayed for me ceaselessly. No matter how much disdain I had for her and how vocal I was about it, she provided for all my needs and *always remained*. Even when I screamed for her to leave me alone, she remained.

Our Lady, Mary, the Mother of God, watched every last ounce of life drain from her Son's body. She witnessed her Son being tortured and killed, knowing that all she could do was *remain*. Her presence was all she could provide for him. As he struggled to breathe, he could simply look at her, knowing that despite the pain and betrayal he had experienced, this beautiful woman, his Mother, loved him. Before her eyes, he could endure anything.

As I sat in the pale light of my friend's room, watching his life slowly slip away, I knew that I was experiencing spiritual motherhood. I appreciated his every breath, remembering his boisterous and childish laugh. I held his aged hands, where bread was transformed into the Body of Christ thousands of times during his priesthood. I moved his body so he could be more comfortable, a body that had spent a lifetime on pilgrimage to his one love, Jesus Christ. When he took his final breath, a silence fell unlike any other. All my years of studying, prayer, and following Mary Magdalene to the hem of our Lady, led me to this moment. Simple, loving presence. Spiritual motherhood poured out of me, and I didn't do anything. This is what Mary did at the foot of the cross. This is what my own mom did as I grew. *Watch and pray.*

During my short time as a consecrated virgin, the lesson I've learned is that spiritual motherhood has far less to do with *doing* than *being*. The Lord continues to deepen my understanding of true feminine presence. Why did my friend ask me to be with him as he died? Because he wanted me to be there. The flawed, emotional Italian woman who didn't understand what to do or how to do it. In order to endure the trials of suffering and death so he could be with our Lord, what he needed from me was simply presence. Spiritual motherhood is inherent in us as women. A beautiful gift from God that allows the feminine heart to grow ever more in love with God and those we encounter.

Yours,

Andrea Polito

> All my years of studying, praying and following Mary Magdalene to the hem of our Lady, led me to this moment. Simple, loving presence. Spiritual motherhood poured out of me, and I didn't do anything. This is what Mary did at the foot of the cross. This is what my own mom did as I grew.
> Watch and pray.
>
> — Andrea Polito

ANDRÉA POLITO is a thirty three-year-old Italian nurse, stumbling, without much ease, through life as a consecrated virgin. Thankfully, she has a great family, wonderful friends, and an endless supply of craft beer from the great city of Denver, Colorado. She was consecrated for the Archdiocese of Denver on the Feast of Saint Mary Magdalene in 2017. She spends her free time reading, biking, and trying to figure out how to be as cool as her fourteen nieces and nephews. She lives an ordinary and boring life, although being a spouse of Christ makes for daily adventures and a track record of 100 percent losses in the "marital disputes" department. She loves talking about consecrated life and exposing other Catholics to its beauty in the Church. All in all she's a normal woman, trying to live in the truth of being chosen by Christ every day.

Reflection Question and Prayer

"Our Lady, Mary, the Mother of God, watched every last ounce of life drain from her Son's body. She witnessed her Son being tortured and killed, knowing that all she could do was *remain*. Her presence was all she could provide for him. As he struggled to breathe, he could simply look at her knowing that despite the pain and betrayal he had experienced, this beautiful woman, his Mother, loved him."

Have you ever been in need of a friend's presence and support in difficult times but instead your friend tried to figure out how to solve your problem? Have you ever been *that* friend? When loved ones are suffering, it can be tempting to see their struggle as a problem to be solved—after all, you love them and you don't want to see them in pain! But sometimes a person may just need you to sit and *be* with them. Is there someone in your life to whom you could be present?

Pray a Hail Mary for those people who feel isolated, and ask that we might recognize more opportunities to just be lovingly present to someone. Then, close with this chapter's petition:

Saint Teresa Benedicta of the Cross, you prayed for, served, and nurtured others up to the moment of your death in a concentration camp. Pray that I may live as lovingly and sacrificially as you did.

II

Create

Singing in the choir at Mass

Allowing God to write the story of your life one decision at a time

Creating a watercolor painting for a sick friend

In this section, we'll examine how femininity can be expressed through artistry, creativity, and being a conduit of God's creative will. In these letters, Catholic women reflect on their creative journeys as women and how they have invited others to know Christ through their lives.

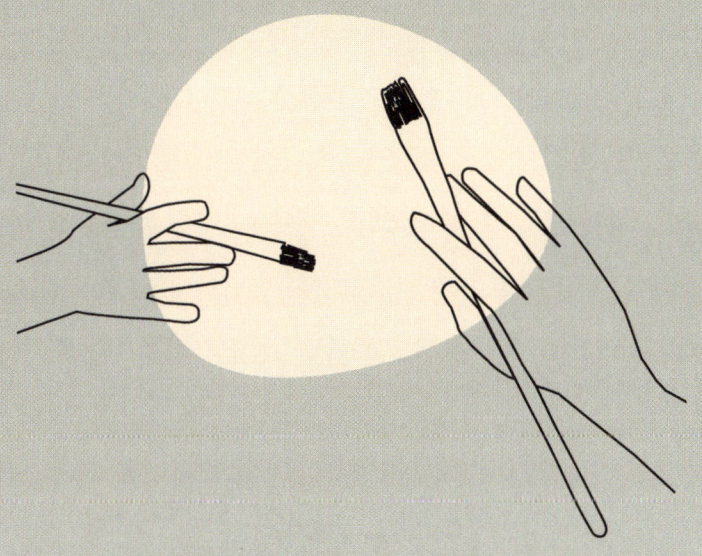

Erica Tighe Campbell

Erica shares how her struggle with alcoholism eventually led her to share her story through her artwork.

Sister Nina Underwood, MMM

Sister Nina shares the surprising adventures she has had simply by corresponding to God's creative will in her life.

Fabiola Garza

Fabiola shares how she strives to bring beauty to every aspect of her life in pursuit of God who is Beauty itself.

Elise Crawford-Gallagher

Elise shares how a disappointing turn in her business led to spiritual renewal and the courage to continue to pursue her dreams.

Gracie Morbitzer

Graceie shares how she has learned to love at all costs with the help of her art and how her paintings show there's room in the Church for everyone.

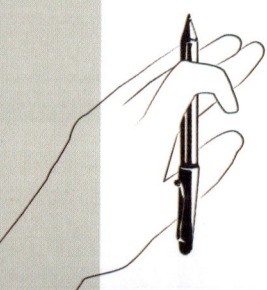

Hildegard of Bingen

Born in 1098 in what is now Germany, Hildegard was placed in the care of a Benedictine abbess when she was only eight. By the time Hildegard was fifteen, she had officially entered the monastery as a novice. Years later, Hildegard would become the abbess of the convent. A renaissance woman (before the Renaissance period even came about), Hildegard was truly a woman ahead of her time. She was a philosopher, composer, theologian, playwright, botanist, and traveling preacher. Her songs and hymns performed in her monasteries are still performed today, and many of her philosophical writings and studies on natural sciences are still in print.

While women in her time were often considered less intelligent than men, Hildegard was widely respected for her impressive intellect, spiritual gifts, and remarkable breadth of knowledge. Sister Prudence Allen, RSM, wrote that Hildegard's work revealed "a genius unparalleled by a woman and matched by very few men up to the twelfth century."[13] Though she was a cloistered nun, and women were not permitted to preach in her time, Hildegard received permission to travel throughout Europe to preach to the faithful. Hildegard's prolific creativity perhaps was rooted in her respect for the harmony and beauty of God's creation. Pope Benedict XVI once wrote that she recognized that "the entire creation is a symphony of the Holy Spirit."[14] In 2012, he named Hildegard a Doctor of the Church.

A women who, against all odds, put her gifts at the service of her community and the Church, Saint Hildegard is a model of the bravery it requires to embrace and develop the unique gifts God has bestowed on each of us. In the coming letters, you'll find examples of women who have courageously learned to embrace their gifts as well as corresponding quotes, questions, and writing-space for you to prayerfully reflect on how you can live this quality out in your own life.

PRAYER TO SAINT HILDEGARD

Saint Hildegard, you used your creative and scientific genius in the service of others. Pray that I may use my gifts to give glory to God and to love my neighbor.

"Your mind is like a wall that changes like clouds and you look around in all directions but you do not have rest. Flee this and remain in tranquility with God and with others, and God will help you in all your tribulations. May God give you his blessing and help you in all that you do."[19]

—Saint Hildegard of Bingen

The Call to Cocreate

To the woman who God is calling,

College was not "the time of my life" as everyone told me it would be. Instead, it left me in a dark depression and disconnected state. I enjoyed my studies but had a hard time connecting with my peers outside of class. After my first year at a small Catholic school that was not the right fit for me, I transferred to a school in Chicago where I did not live on the campus where everyone else made friends. To try to fit in, I started drinking alcohol to take away the social anxiety I was experiencing. Drinking, however, was not a safe experience for me. I almost always woke up the next day in a cloud of depression and disconnection from myself.

After graduating from college, I took all the money I had been saving and backpacked through Europe alone for six weeks. During college, the one place I had found some solace was at the Art Institute of Chicago so I visited every art museum I could find. Across an ocean, in cities where I didn't speak the same language as the people around me, I sat in front of original Van Goghs, Monets, and Rembrandts. And, for the first time in a long time, I didn't feel so alone. Each painting was a tiny light of hope into the inner turmoil of darkness that gripped me. Through those tiny paint strokes laid over a hundred years before, God's heart was able to reach me.

A few months later, I left Europe for Brazil where I would live for eighteen months as a volunteer. The organization I worked for had a mission to be a heart, nothing but a heart. Our mission was to be like Mary at the foot of the cross. I thought that a life spent in service of others would bring me closer to God and teach me how to better love. The friends I made in the Brazilian people did bring me a joy I hadn't experienced in many years. The hours I spent sitting on the floor of our simple chapel in front of the tabernacle and the hours I spent on the couches of elderly women over a *cafezinho* (a little coffee with lots of sugar) was a time of deep uncovering—a healing. My job in our village was to care for the local schoolhouse and the children who visited it. I quickly noticed that beyond regular academics, the children I met were also in need of emotional healing from the trauma they already had experienced in their young lives. So, from my limited resources (and supplies friends sent from back home), we began studying different artists from around the world. We practiced techniques like they used: painting upside down like Michelangelo and making a big mess sloshing paint around like Pollock. As they learned to express themselves artistically, I saw tiny transformations in the children. They began to keep trying when they didn't like the first result, and they learned to admire beauty.

When I returned to the States, my old friend depression greeted me. I fumbled around, feeling out of place in New York City. I had decided to move there because the organization I had worked with in Brazil also had a house in some projects in Brooklyn with a bed that I could rent. I thought it would be a good way to transition. But even though I was living in a very old rectory building and sleeping in bunk beds with a couple of female roommates, life in New York felt so very foreign. How could I live in such prosperity when I knew there was so much poverty elsewhere? How could I relate to new friends who were already in their full-time jobs post college and had no idea what it's like to visit Dona Virginha who lived down off the railroad tracks? I again took solace in drinking alcohol to escape my feelings, and I found myself even more miserable than before my time in Brazil.

Over a short time, all the inner joy I had found in Brazil began to slip away. What I thought would bring total healing—living fully in service of others—ended up being a bit more a form of escapism. I hadn't reached the root of my depression quite yet. I felt like I was moving through molasses with a dark tint over the world. I worked as a nanny for several families, and while I loved the kids, it was very lonely work. I was so worried about what I was going to do for the rest of my life, where to find meaning, and how to cope with the feeling of dread that greeted me each day. I remember hanging out with friends while everyone was having a good time, but I was unable to be present and to truly enjoy myself.

As I sank to the bottom of my sadness, I pushed my arm above water for help, and miraculously Father Michael was there to grab my hand. For Lent, I decided that I would wake up early to go to daily Mass. The first week, I asked the priest if I would be able to go to confession. After Mass, we met in the sacristy and I cried. I told him of my despair and all the things I was feeling so much shame about. He asked if I had a spiritual director, and I said no but that I had been praying for one! So he told me to come back again the following Tuesday, and he would be my spiritual director.

Father Michael was a sigh of relief in my life. In our weekly meetings, he began to untangle the misconceptions I had about life and God. Over many months he helped me to see that alcohol was hindering me from reaching any kind of happiness and derailing any healing that had been taking place. It took me six months to actually believe him, but I eventually got outside help to get sober. But letting go of my old coping mechanisms was not as easy as just quitting alcohol. Even sober I was still left with all of the reasons why I had taken to drinking in the first place. The cold New York winter nights were long, and I needed something to fill my time. I recalled that artistic beauty had been a light for me and for the children in Brazil, and I wondered if I could find some joy in actually being on the side of creation.

I remembered that my mother had taught me calligraphy as a child, and I thought it might be a good art form to practice in my small apartment.

Calligraphy soon became a meditative practice for me. The way the ink flowed out of the nib onto the paper, the hair-thin lines as I lifted my hand just slightly. In the process of keeping my hand and my mind busy, I was able to connect my heart to God's presence. My mind that had been constantly overthinking and filled with anxiety would quiet down, and I could hear God's voice whispering, "You are good, you have something to offer, I love you, I need you." In this state of calm, I was able to go to sleep more easily. And the next day, it gave me something to look forward to—it had been so long since I had looked forward to something! I looked forward to putting in the practice, to improving, and to learning more. I looked forward to the relief as the meditative movements carried me through my worries and anxieties.

Calligraphy wasn't exactly intuitive, and I was terrible at it for months, but I didn't care about the end result. I just cared about the process. Once I got a better hang of it (okay, let's be real, I was still terrible), I started lettering quotes that spoke to my heart and eventually posted them to my social media accounts. I wrote captions that shared my heart to go along with the quotes and what I was going through in my human experience. And my art started to resonate with others. Just as the beautiful art in the many museums I had visited had resonated so deeply within me, these tiny quotes written by hand were speaking to a person on the other side of the screen.

This is what I had always longed for—connection with another person. When I'm stuck in my depression, connection is impossible for me. The joy I had found in Brazil as a volunteer wasn't so much about doing something for someone but in connecting with them. I began to find such joy in creating beauty and in taking part in the creation of beauty. My art taught me how to be a cocreator with the Creator. In this act of creation—pen and ink to paper—I learned that I needed to embrace cocreating my life with God. The life I had longed for was not going to happen by praying while sitting back and expecting God to come in with a magic wand like a genie and grant me all my wishes. Nor was life something I had to figure out in despair, completely on my own. My life then became both engulfed in prayerful connection with God and in taking action to engage in activities that brought my soul to life.

As my soul awakened, I learned more and more about the woman God had created me and was calling me to be. I began to find value in who I was and in who I was becoming. I learned of the beauty that it is to simply be a woman—full of compassion, joy, vulnerability, strength, and love. I quit trying to hide, and the light within me was able to shine in places of shame and self-hatred.

Beauty saves the world (and saved my world) because it fosters hope and connection—two things we need when life's lights dim. I never anticipated what the Lord would do with my hand. Today, creating is my full-time job that I hope inspires others to seek healing and to grab someone else's hand in times of despair. I hope it encourages others to live fully, to find their deep calling, and not to let suffering have the last word.

Cocreation might look different for you than it does for me. God calls us, as women, in so many unique ways to join him in creating. We see this reality in motherhood, the greatest way we foster life (either through our wombs or by loving those who have been given to us). We cocreate in the meals we make for others, in the way we decorate our homes, in the clothes we choose to wear. We are cocreators in the stories we write and the way we love. God beckons you, too, to join him in creating the life for which you long. My art has become a way for me to tell the story of a God who never gave up on me, a God who delights in me, a God who loves me just as he loves all of his creation—including you. He waits for you to call on him and to ask for the guidance to live a life worthy of his calling.

All my love and companionship,

Erica

ERICA TIGHE CAMPBELL is the founder of Be A Heart, a design company that shares the continual cycle of life, death, and resurrection in our lives. Through her art, Erica hopes to promote the joy and love experienced in a life with Christ. She is originally from Phoenix and has had the privilege of living in Chicago, Salvador da Bahia, Brazil, Brooklyn, and Los Angeles before landing in San Antonio with her husband, Paul, and their child. You can find her at beaheart.com and on social media at @ericatighecampbell and @beaheartdesign.

As my soul awakened, I learned more and more about the woman God created me and was calling me to be. I began to find value in who I was and who I was becoming. I learned of the beauty that it is to simply be a woman — full of compassion, joy, vulnerability, strength, and love. I quit trying to hide, and the light within me was able to shine in places of shame and self-hatred.

Xo,
erica

Reflection Question and Prayer

"Beauty saves the world (and saved my world) because it fosters hope and connection—two things we need when life's lights dim. I never anticipated what the Lord would do with my hand. Today, creating is my full-time job that I hope inspires others to seek healing and to grab someone else's hand in times of despair. I hope it encourages others to live fully, to find their deep calling, and not to let suffering have the last word."

Take a moment to brainstorm how you can foster hope and connection through beauty in your life. How can you cultivate beauty right where you are? It could be as simple as lighting a candle, meditating on a psalm, or texting a note of encouragement to a friend.

Pray a Hail Mary for those who are lonely and those who struggle with despair. Pray that beauty may shine a light of hope into their lives. Then, close with this section's petition:

Saint Hildegard, you used your creative and scientific genius in the service of others. Pray that I may use my gifts to give glory to God and to love my neighbor.

Faith, Fairytales, and Beauty

Dear Sister,

One thing I cherish more than anything else is imagination. When I was little, I remember watching *Snow White* for the first time. The fairytale world onscreen seemed so magical that I thought, "God has to exist." I grasped that creation could not just be the random result of a cosmic explosion. That moment two things were born in my heart: A desire to know God and a desire to make art. Like twins they continue to walk side by side, sometimes working together and at other times simply keeping each other company.

A third desire came when I was a little older, but it was a natural progression of the ideas that delighted me. The desire was to be in a fairytale. Grappling with how to pursue these desires has been both a heartbreaking and a thrilling adventure. At times I've let the world tell me who I should be and what I should want. Sometimes I was afraid that if I followed Christ, I would have to give up my love of movies and happily-ever-afters. I thought that if I gave my life over to God, I would lose the things I loved. Instead, he ended up purifying those desires so they would compete no longer with his place in my heart. And then, I was surprised to find, I could enjoy the things I loved all the more. God has called me to a higher adventure and a more enduring fairy-tale ending.

Until college, however, I kept God in a box. It's what was done. Growing up, one didn't talk about religion in school. It wasn't polite. But I prayed and talked to God and sometimes wrote down my prayers. I was a naturally spiritual kid with a strong conscience. The very first sin I remember committing involved a kindergarten art project. Of course. Because art was the most important thing in my life because I loved it, and it was one thing I was good at. That day we were tasked with creating a caterpillar out of two green strips of paper. I placed one strip on top of the other in a V-shape, and then slowly folded one piece over the other, over and over until it looked like an accordion. I looked at mine. It looked alright. Then I glanced at the girl's next to me. It was so much better. I waited for her to leave her desk, and the

> "Not all are called to be artists in the specific sense of the term. Yet, as Genesis has it, all men and women are entrusted with the task of crafting their own life: in a certain sense, they are to make of it a work of art, a masterpiece."[16]
>
> —Saint John Paul II

moment she did I grabbed her caterpillar and threw it in the trash. That, and my seething jealousy, is all I remember. I recall experiencing the exact same feeling of jealousy in the first grade. This time, I left the drawing in question alone, but I nevertheless felt a strong need to be better. To be the best. Even if I wasn't aware of it, my sense of self-worth was becoming intertwined with how good my art was compared to others' art. Nobody ever told me that my worth came from God alone. So for a long time I didn't even conceive of that possibility.

Ever since I can remember, I have wanted to work for Disney. In a diary I started when I was ten years old, I glued my school picture inside the front jacket and wrote underneath:

Fabiola

10 years old

When I grow up I want to be a Disney animator

I watched all the Disney movies and knew all the songs by heart. I drew many of the characters with colored pencils, and my mom still recalls the many hours I spent sketching. My love for imaginary worlds and stories made me an avid reader as well, and great at pretending. Depending on the day, I would ask my mom to call me by a different character's name. One day I was "Ariel"; another day "Alice."

Alice in Wonderland was my favorite. I was drawn to the idea that she had explored a secret place. I walked around school with a giant, illustrated copy of *Alice's Adventures in Wonderland*. I asked my mom to sew me her costume (not from the Disney movie version, surprisingly, but from a TV miniseries that came out in 1985). I would compel my father to film me reenacting the miniseries verbatim in my backyard. The other characters from the show were played by my plush toys. To this day, I lament the loss of that videotape.

When *Beauty and the Beast* came out in 1990, fairytales, princesses, and happily-ever-afters began to really seep into my subconscious. Had I known then that God is the source of all joy and the mirror by which to judge all my desires, this wouldn't have been dangerous. But I didn't know that, and soon the belief took hold that I would only be happy if I were a beautiful princess with a fairytale prince to love me. The idea of a fairytale life became my idol before I even knew what an idol was. All my favorite things were in the wrong place: the fairytale was my end, art was my measuring stick, and the Lord was unreachable.

Slowly, I became a woman I didn't like and didn't know how to help. Critical of my looks, I avoided bathing suits, and I constantly dieted. I worried that men wouldn't like me if they didn't think I was beautiful. I spent hours reading fairy tales, dreaming and hoping that my life could be like the lives of the brave girls in the books. When I entered college and people's talent exceeded my own, I fought to keep up my self-esteem. Envy was pernicious, and I couldn't stop comparing myself to those around me. I still loved drawing; I spent hours creating my own versions of fairy tales and characters and dreamed of working for a big animation company. But I also was unhappy.

Then, when I was most confused about life and my identity, I found myself in a situation where I was forced to talk about God and my faith. Compelled by my strong desire to find true love, I was dating a man who was Christian but not Catholic. We argued about the faith, so I began to study more about it. As I grappled with the tension and breakdown of my relationship, I sought refuge in the wisdom of the Church. More versed than most cradle Catholics in the faith, I still was never taught that we are most free when we center our identity in the Lord. I began frequenting daily Mass and adoration, and I started to fall in love with Jesus. For the first time in my life, I had found another way to find joy. The box I had placed God in had opened—for good.

The twisted paths of my heart and mind slowly and painfully unraveled (and no doubt will continue to until I leave this world). After I realized how deeply the Lord loves me, what surprised me most was that I still got to keep all the things I had loved before in my life. As I drew closer to God, I feared that I would have to stop making art that wasn't explicitly religious. But he didn't ask me to do that. I can draw Saint John Paul II *and* Mickey Mouse. The state of my soul and my care for others are what's most important. But I also always listen to God to see if he's asking me to do a project for him.

God's divine imagination brought
the entire universe into being.
My imagination is minute
compared to the creator's, but
my desire to give birth to
something new comes from him.

Fabiola Garza

During my last year of college, he placed a seed of inspiration in me to write and illustrate a children's book on the life of Pope John Paul II. I had never been so uplifted by a man's relationship with God. John Paul II's *life* was a fairy tale. The pain, the victory, the love—all the elements were there. He lost all his family members by the age of nineteen and lived through Nazi and Communist occupations. Yet he lived with a love and vibrancy that only God could have supplied. His life story helped me to realize that the real happily-ever-after is to end up in God's arms. I wanted others to know his story that had so transformed me. When the book was published, it didn't feel like I had switched from doing worldly art to the work of God because all art speaks of his eternal beauty. I also didn't feel like I was leaving God behind when I accepted a position at the Walt Disney Company that same year.

Now I spend my days drawing Disney princesses and myriad other beloved characters. Through prayer, I've allowed the Lord to constantly challenge where I'm placing my identity. I've found that my energy to make and create beautiful things grows when I no longer waste time seeking the world's approval. Now, the entire world is my canvas—I want to make everything beautiful. As an expression of my joy, I love curating my wardrobe and creating a whimsical environment around me. My office, for instance, looks like a magic woodland. I still love the idea of being a princess. Though some might say it's a childish image, it's one I've embraced wholeheartedly—I'm a princess who fights for something greater than herself.

God's divine imagination brought the entire universe into being. My imagination is minute compared to the Creator's, but my desire to give birth to something new comes from him. This deep desire also comes from my feminine heart, and I fulfill it by creating beautiful stories and images. In the end, though I hope to make something beautiful with my hands, I most of all want to do something beautiful with my heart.

Art might seem useless to our everyday survival, until we realize that beauty is a gateway to the eternal. When we are surrounded by works that make us wonder, we walk toward the truth all the more.

Love,

Fabiola

FABIOLA GARZA is a character artist for Disney Creative Group. She also writes and illustrates. Her first award-winning book is *A Boy Who Became Pope: The Story of Saint John Paul II*. Fabiola is an avid reader of everything from young adult fantasy novels to the writings of Saint Francis de Sales. Originally from Mexico, she has traveled the world since early childhood; she has lived in Turkey and Colombia and currently lives in the United States. She received a BFA in illustration from Rhode Island School of Design. Forever trying to be a "saint warrior princess," she helps teach the faith to high schoolers at her local parish and is faithful to ballroom dance classes every week.

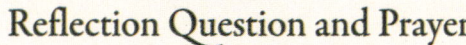

Reflection Question and Prayer

"Sometimes I was afraid that if I followed Christ, I would have to give up my love of movies and happily-ever-afters. I thought that if I gave my life over to God, I would lose the things I loved."

Are there hobbies you enjoy or dreams you have that you feel you'd have to give up if you really pursued a life with Christ? Sometimes, God does call us to give up those things out of love for us, but more often than not, the dreams and passions we have come from deeper desires that he's placed on each of our hearts. As she shared in her letter, Fabiola thought she would have to give up her love of movies and fairytales, when in reality, God wanted to purify those passions and lead her to something greater. God is calling you to invite him into every corner of your heart. Reflect on what parts of your life—whether intentionally or not—you might be holding back from God today.

Then, pray a Hail Mary asking God to help you to live your deepest desires in union with his creative love. Then, close with this section's petition:

Saint Hildegard, you used your creative and scientific genius in the service of others. Pray that I may use my gifts to give glory to God and to love my neighbor.

The Adventure of Service

Dear Reader,

I'm delighted to share my journey of the last fifty years with you. Both an exterior journey to many parts of Africa and, more importantly, an interior journey. In my more than fifty years as a missionary, I have learned to trust and cling to God, father and mother to us all.[20]

As far back as I can remember, even as a very young child, I felt both adventurous and yet held in a peaceful Presence. I dreamed of being a nurse and missionary—but certainly not a nun. I wasn't brought up in an overly pious home, but I was blessed with parents who were hardworking and had great faith. They made sacrifices to send their seven children to Catholic schools. My aunts and great grandmother were also influential figures in my life; they showed me that holiness is found in the ordinary, daily living of one's faith. My parents often sponsored and supported causes that directly assisted the poor and prioritized serving those less fortunate. So, at a young age, through the example of my mother and father, through the religious sisters in school and in films, and through reading stories of the needs of the poor and sick in faraway places, I felt drawn to service. I wanted to help, but I didn't know how.

When I was in high school, my older sister, Pat, entered religious life. At that time, I had no desire to do the same, but the seed of a call was planted in my heart. Yet I resisted, as I did not want to be a "nun." Time passed, and I found myself living next door to the Medical Missionaries of Mary in Winchester, Massachusetts. I was drawn by the openness and hospitality of the sisters. They also had a gorgeous German Shepherd called Shep, and I was (and still am!) crazy about dogs. Not knowing what to do next, I decided to try other religious missionary orders. When I was not accepted, I was delighted. I thought, "Well, that must not be God's will for me." The urging of the Holy Spirit, however, led me to ask to enter to the Medical Missionaries of Mary, and to my surprise, I was warmly welcomed and accepted by our foundress, Mother Mary Martin. I then began a sincere discerning process, and with the help of the wise women who surrounded me, I became sure I had a vocation to the missionary life.

After several years in formation, I felt a profound sense of Holy Mystery. This Mystery encompassed me, and I experienced something of a conversion to acceptance of religious life, despite my feelings of unworthiness. The Holy Spirit had given me a great desire to see and seek God with all my heart. In those early years of formation, I developed a longing for a deep relationship with God and valued prayer and spiritual reading. I also realized that the best way for me to help the neediest in the world was to embrace my religious order's healing charism: "That they might have life and have it more abundantly" (Jn 10:10).

Religious sisters in the Medical Missionaries of Mary are sent where the need is greatest, and human development is paramount. In view of this, I was sent to study nursing at the International Missionary Training Hospital in Ireland. I was happily engaged in my nursing studies when my life met a sudden curve in the road. Someone had donated a plane to the congregation, and I was asked if I would like to fly it—to become a pilot! I would be running a transport system in an area in Kenya that had no roads. So off I went to Dublin Airport and began flying lessons with an Aer Lingus pilot. Eight months later, I qualified and was on my way to the Turkana Desert in northern Kenya where our sisters were responding to a severe drought and famine that had begun in the 1960s and continued on and off until the 1980s.

In Kenya, I joined a team that included other religious sisters from my congregation, nongovernmental workers, and the local Church. We especially worked closely with the Flying Doctors Service of East Africa, an organization that provided us with support and financial assistance.

During one of the most challenging and fulfilling times of my life, we were able to bring much needed relief to thousands of nomadic people scattered over an area of 32,000 square miles. Every two weeks, I would make the rounds in our plane to visit the mission stations that dotted the desert area. Several religious sisters from my congregation who were also doctors and nurses would accompany me to the dispensaries and hospitals. We would bring much-needed food, mail, and medicine to the people in the area.

We all felt the Lord's protection during these difficult times. Sometimes we had difficulty transporting patients to a specialist hospital in Nairobi. Most people from the areas we were helping had never flown before. Most people got into the plane without issue, but others were terrified. One sick, older man was so upset when we took off that he tried to open the cabin door and jump out at 7,000-feet altitude. Another time, I faced the hardship of pranging (crashing) the plane I was flying. I was stuck for two days without food in the desert until I was rescued by the Kenya Air Force. Naturally, that was incredibly challenging, but I embraced the opportunity to meet a lot of local people I wouldn't otherwise have had the chance to meet.

In the early 90s, I was privileged to work in ministry with the Maryknoll Sisters in southern Sudan. We ministered to the poorest of the poor in war-torn southern Sudan, providing primary healthcare and health education. We also empowered women's groups to set up small businesses to sustain their families. We did all this while working closely with and in support of the local Church. One month into my stay, I was returning from Juba with another Maryknoll sister to our mission station. When we arrived, a group of SPLA rebels (Sudan's People's Liberation Army) was looting our mission for food and medicine. They shot at us and then took us hostage. The rebels transported us through the bush to a camp of about one thousand other SPLA rebels. There we joined another small group of hostages and spent a week at the camp.

I learned so much while I was a hostage about living in insecurity and uncertainty. It was a real lesson in solidarity with those who suffer the atrocities of war. I also identified more with the brave faithful people of southern Sudan, including many women, who have lived amid war for over four decades. After this ordeal, along with the other Maryknoll sister, I was expelled as a *persona non grata* and told to leave the country. The bishop in Sudan advised us to go to Kenya and to wait until he invited us back. I returned to southern Sudan within a month. We continued working in public health care and health education in southern Sudan, ministering in the camps and daily outstations in the surrounding area.

After my experience in southern Sudan, I was asked to relieve one of my religious sisters, who worked in the Kibera slums in Nairobi, Kenya. There I began working with people living with HIV/AIDS. Working with HIV/AIDS patients made me more aware of the way we discriminate and shun the people who most need our help and support. During this time, I felt particularly called to accompany those facing death. I also was gifted with an opportunity to undertake the eighty-mile journey up and down Mount Kilimanjaro (a real "mountaintop" experience and another awesome story!).

After spending most of my adult life overseas helping the poor and sick in Africa, I was then presented with a new challenge. I was called home. My mother was elderly and unwell and needed my support and care. I lived with her and also helped out as a pastoral minister in the local hospital in Portsmouth, New Hampshire. My time in Nairobi prepared me to minister to the sick and dying, and it also led me to reflect on each stage of my life. I thought about how God had led me on paths unknown and not chosen by me, but each piece prepared me for the next step. God always was right by my side, holding my hand on the journey of life.

As I was caring for my Mum, my sister, Terry, came to look after her so I could take a short break. In response to a famine crisis, I volunteered to go to Niger in West Africa with three other Medical Missionaries of Mary. We worked with *GOAL*, an international charity dedicated to alleviating the sufferings of the poorest of the poor. Seeing starving people was incredibly difficult, but when we brought them food, their happiness was well worth the terrible heat and travel conditions. In spite of the hardship and misery we faced, my return to Africa was very welcome. It felt like going home. I remember that period in my life with deep gratitude.

The religious sisters of the Medical Missionaries of Mary are called to an extraordinary adventure. Our lives are a faith-filled "yes" that like Mary's is uttered in response to God's continual call. My life has been an extraordinary adventure of faith despite and also because of the many disappointments, discouragements, and dangers. Gratitude fills my heart as I look back on my fifty-year journey with the Medical Missionaries of Mary. I could not have found a more adventurous and extraordinary life. Or I should say, dear reader, the life found me. As a Catholic woman of faith, I am God's woman, and mission is everywhere as I continue to say "yes" to life. May life give you as much joy and peace as has been granted to me.

Every blessing,

Nina

Sister Nina Underwood, MMM, was born and raised in Boston, Massachusetts. After entering the Medical Missionaries of Mary, she trained as a nurse only then to be asked to become a pilot! For many years, she flew a medical supply plan in the remote desert area of Turkana in Kenya, East Africa. Later she did pastoral ministry in refugee camps in South Sudan and then returned to Kenya to work with HIV/AIDS patients in Nairobi. After returning to the United States to care for her mother, she undertook massage therapy and chaplaincy work in New Hampshire. Nina presently lives in Somerville, Massachusetts, and recently celebrated fifty years of vowed religious life. To learn more about the Medical Missionaries of Mary, you can visit mmmworldwide.org.

I learned so much while I was
a hostage about living in insecurity
and uncertainty. It was a real
lesson in solidarity with those
who suffer the atrocities of war

Nina Underwood mmm

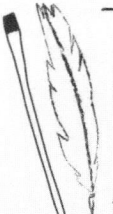

Reflection Question and Prayer

"I could not have found a more adventurous and extraordinary life. Or I should say, dear reader, the life found me. As a Catholic woman of faith, I am God's woman, and mission is everywhere as I continue to say 'yes' to life."

Take a moment to reflect on your life. How has it been an adventure with God? Are there ways you could be more open to the creative adventure of his grace? How is God calling you to use your gifts to serve those in need?

Pray a Hail Mary for all those who suffer in war-torn countries and for those in captivity. Then, close with this section's petition:

Saint Hildegard, you used your creative and scientific genius in the service of others. Pray that I may use my gifts to give glory to God and to love my neighbor.

The Courage
to Keep Going

Dear Sisters,

One late Friday summer evening, I sat weeping in a gorgeous Franciscan monastery chapel. I watched as sunbeams streaked through a window and fell across the wooden tabernacle in front of me.

"Why in the world do I think I can do this? Did I hear your calling correctly? Am I on the right path?!"

My company, RINGLET, had just lost a bid for a huge client, and I was devastated. Weeks earlier, when presenting to the potential client, I had felt like our companies were a great match and that they'd inevitably hire us. They would have been the biggest client we had ever booked. My team and I were excited by this project's potential and knew it was a huge opportunity. I was sure this specific work was the Lord's will. Instead, they emailed back a week later saying they had decided to go in a different direction.

I was stunned. It felt like I had been hit by a truck. Worse yet, this rejection came at the end of a monthlong dry stint, one of our slowest sales months to date. My team and I were stressed, exhausted, and discouraged. The tunnel toward our ambitions had gone completely dark. I felt so lost. Had I misunderstood my mission as an entrepreneur? Did the Lord want me to start this business in the first place? Why was this happening to us?

As I sat in the chapel, I traced my memories back to the beginning. Although I'm the daughter of an entrepreneur, I never had dreamed of owning my own business. Growing up, I never was focused when it came to my career. Unlike my siblings and many of my peers who knew from a young age what they wanted to do when they grew up, I jumped from one passion to the next. In high school, I loved acting and was convinced I was going to live a life on the stage. In college, I fell in love with philosophy, and post-college I devoured theological truths in a master's program.

Midway through my master's, I decided to intentionally think about what I wanted to do "when I grew up" and became enamored of the developing trends in digital marketing and social media. So I pivoted one more time and went on to study and receive a master's in communication. Then, after years of working at Catholic nonprofits and for-profit public relations agencies, I decided to take the leap and launch my own marketing agency.

I started my own company because I saw a huge need in my hometown area of Baltimore and Washington, D.C. A growing community of women-owned businesses desperately needed resources, media education, and marketing. But they didn't have the capital to hire expensive public relations and marketing agencies or even a handful of freelancers to complete the various tasks they needed to get their businesses off the ground. I knew many women entrepreneurs with a great desire to create but with fear and uncertainty around how to make it happen. I felt called to use my creativity and talents in communications to serve these growing needs. So I started my own company to offer a solution. I wanted to walk beside women as I strategized with them and pushed them to dream bigger and reach further.

I wish I could tell you that the first time I felt desolate about my business was when I was sitting in that Franciscan chapel, but it wasn't. When I started RINGLET, I was not prepared for the constant emotional highs and lows of owning a business. One day I feel like I am totally aligned with the Lord's will for me and empowering the women in my community; the next I'm convinced that this crazy dream is never going to work. So why keep going?

As I looked upon Jesus in the tabernacle of that quiet chapel that summer evening, a thought occurred to me:

Why do I believe I should be exempt from the cross? For centuries, saints have given their lives because they believed in their life's mission: to bear Christ to the world. Successful businesses are not made overnight. Impact happens only with patience. So why was I sitting here feeling sorry for myself because things got tough? Now, in all fairness, in that moment, I was absolutely crushed. I felt invalidated, weak, and exhausted. But Christ held my heart, and in his kind manner, he told me to *keep going.*

Encouraging us to persevere, the author of Hebrews writes, "Let us run with perseverance the race that is set before us, looking to Jesus the pioneer and perfecter of our faith, who for the sake of the joy that was set before him endured the cross, disregarding its shame, and has taken his seat at the right hand of the throne of God" (Heb 12:1–2, NRSV). As twenty-first-century women, it's so easy to give up on our dreams. We're often told we're at the same time too much and too little. We're too ambitious, but we don't earn enough. We're pretty, but not pretty enough. We hear a small quiet voice whispering our hopes and dreams, but we instantly think that those dreams are beyond impossible. Or after a few months (or years) of trying to achieve our goals, we become tired and lose focus.

From years of falling down and getting up again, I've learned that this call to "keep going" is intrinsic to my vocation as a wife, mother, and entrepreneur. I'm not a physical mother. Yet, my businesses are a result of cocreating with God. Every day, I must rely on God to persevere in the task he has set before me: to create a business that brings him to the world through our services and the Christ-like way we treat our clients. Every interaction I have with an employee or client is an opportunity to introduce them to Christ. When I feel discouraged and worried, I lean into Jesus'

You can do hard things.
You can be audacious and courageous.
You can embrace the evangelical maternal
nature of your womanhood and radically
change the world.
Don't be afraid, sister, you were
made for this.

♡ Elise
Crawford
Gallagher

words, *keep going*. Through daily Mass, praying the Divine Mercy chaplet, and going to adoration, I feel Christ's encouragement, his gentle hand moving me forward—even when I can't see the future clearly.

Throughout his pontificate, Saint Pope John Paul II emphasized the Church's need to raise up a powerful and holy generation of laypeople. Women specifically have a call to lean into our motherhood, spiritual and physical, to bring about a new evangelization. In *Mulieris Dignitatem*, John Paul wrote, "*The motherhood* of every woman, understood in the light of the Gospel, is similarly not only 'of flesh and blood': it expresses a profound *'listening to the word of the living God'* and a readiness to 'safeguard' this Word, which is the word of eternal life" (see Jn 6:68).[21] Whether we are single, married, consecrated single, or discerning, we are all called to motherhood. We were each created to answer the deep longings of our hearts to create beauty and to radiate the truth of God in our lives.

I was first introduced to this concept of spiritual motherhood when I was studying abroad in Rome as a sophomore in college. I was discerning religious life and had decided to break up with my boyfriend a few months earlier. I felt vulnerable and lost. One cold winter day after Mass, I was walking across the Ponte Milvio bridge when I heard a small, quiet voice speak to my heart, "You are my little mother." It's taken me years to unpack that statement, but that particular moment propelled my whole future forward. It led me to my vocation of marriage (to the boyfriend I had broken up with when I was in Rome!). And eventually it led me to start my own business.

As women, our spiritual motherhood is the bridge that connects our faith to those around us. When we live our spiritual maternity in union with God, we bring Christ into the world through our daily lives: through our care for families and friends, our work, our businesses, our conversations with coworkers, and our social media posts. When we courageously embrace the truth of our identity as women, that we are daughters of the King of the Universe and communicators of the Truth, we seize our strength. This call isn't easy. As I've experienced time and time again, living out one's call from God isn't for the faint of heart. The devil will try to discourage us and convince us it isn't worth it. He'll try to lead us to believe that what we're doing isn't of any worth. In the face of the devil's wiles, have the audacity to believe that you are worthy of the great calling that God has placed on your heart.

At a million points along this journey, it would have made sense for me to shut down my business: I was late for payroll, I had an unhappy client, my business model had to change yet again. I've had to humble myself and ask for help and guidance. I've had to look fear in the face and decide to move forward anyway. Through all the challenges, the desire to live the greatness to which God calls me propelled me forward and helped me to persevere.

Dear sister, have the audacity and the courage to keep going. Be bold enough to believe that the dreams the Lord places in your heart are a path to change in the world. Your dreams can be empowering; they also can be an invitation to encounter the Cross. Your dreams are not only how you are called to reflect Christ's love to the world, they also are the place where you will share in Christ's suffering and redemption.

When you're misunderstood, *keep going.*

When you feel vulnerable, *keep going.*

When you feel all is lost and can't see the next step, *keep going.*

When you're completely drained of energy, *keep going.*

When you dare to try again when you've failed repeatedly, *keep going.*

When you see no hope, *keep going.*

You can do hard things. You can be audacious and courageous. You can embrace the evangelical, maternal nature of your womanhood and radically change the world. Don't be afraid, sister, *you were made for this.*

Love,

Elise

ELISE CRAWFORD GALLAGHER is the founder and CEO of RINGLET, a digital marketing agency based in Washington, D.C., that serves women-owned businesses. Elise graduated from The Catholic University of America and received her master's in Communication from Johns Hopkins University. Along with Emma Moran, Elise founded Catholic Women in Business (CWIB) whose mission is to provide Catholic women business leaders and entrepreneurs with the needed educational and spiritual resources to excel in their vocations to business. Elise married her college sweetheart; they live in Maryland. She is so grateful to her husband, parents, sister, and brothers for their abundant encouragement, love, and support.

Reflection Question and Prayer

"As women, our spiritual motherhood is the bridge that connects our faith to those around us. When we live our spiritual maternity in union with God, we bring Christ into the world through our daily lives: through our care for families and friends, our work, our businesses, our conversations with coworkers, and our social media posts. When we courageously embrace the truth of our identity as women, that we are daughters of the King of the Universe and communicators of the Truth, we seize our strength."

When was the last time something you planned didn't go as anticipated? How did you recover? Reflect on what graces God brought as a result of that situation.

Pray a Hail Mary for a growth in fortitude and perseverance. Then, close with this section's petition:

Saint Hildegard, you used your creative and scientific genius in the service of others. Pray that I may use my gifts to give glory to God and to love my neighbor.

After having known people who felt turned from Christianity by Christians, I now do all I can to act in constant mercy, honesty, & love.

Gracia Morkitzer

The Church:
Home for the Outcast

Hi,

I'm Gracie. I was born across the street from Golden Gate Park in San Francisco. The place where Janis Joplin, George Harrison, and Jefferson Airplane once played. The place where hippies still thrive to this day. I'm passionate about the environment. I can't help but dance when music is good, eat when food smells great, and lounge outside for entire days and nights when it's summer. I never miss Dave Matthews when he's in town. I could spend my whole paycheck thrifting. And my dream is to one day go to the Oscars.

I also really love Jesus.

When I was introducing myself for the first time in art school, I said all that except the last line. When I started college, I was so excited to finally meet other people like me. People who loved to get out and travel; people who had new, big ideas; people who weren't easy to find in the places I had been before. I was so excited to be around people who would understand my font obsession, know how to use screen printing equipment, and share my love for Marc Chagall. I was excited to be around people with whom I had so much in common. Except my faith.

Virtually no faith community existed at my college. As a result, I was scared to share my faith; I worried it would separate me from the groups I wanted to be in. And, honestly, it did. In conversations, I soon realized just how far I was willing to go to distance myself from my faith. When I heard things I didn't agree with, I would just nod my head and remain silent. I thought, "How can I speak up when everyone else in the room is so knowledgeable and passionate about opinions that oppose my own?" I wondered what might happen if I disagreed out loud with my friends.

At the same time I was making the transition to college, all sorts of things were billowing out of the news onto social media suggesting that Christians are bigoted and hateful. I knew I didn't fit that description. I also knew many people in college who had been hurt by other Christians who had acted uncharitably toward them. It devastated me. But to be perceived as hateful just because I was a Christian was also frustrating and hurtful.

Even if people didn't make such extreme assumptions about me because I was a Christian, many still assumed I wouldn't drink, wouldn't listen to anything other than Christian rock, and wouldn't understand anything not G-rated. People seemed to think Christians were never fun, interesting, or adventurous. The accusing and assuming voices around me were so loud that I didn't think I could do anything to change the situation. I believed I had to choose between being labeled and misunderstood or quiet about my faith.

Then, gradually, a random painting began to fix my problem. I wanted an image of my faith in my dorm room but in a style I enjoyed rather than traditional religious art. So I painted Jesus dressed in a white T-shirt onto a piece of wood. I also made a painting of Mary in a jacket. Then I painted my Confirmation patron saint, Saint Genevieve, with freckles and braids. Eventually, I shared these images online, and my Catholic friends and family back home started to ask for modern renditions of their own patron saints. I was up for it. I had fun finding weird, ugly pieces of wood at thrift stores and turning them into something cool.

I had always been so fascinated by the saints, and as I painted them, I was beginning to realize why. As I researched each saint, I realized that they were like the pieces of wood on which I painted. They were all different ages. Some had marks and wounds. They were various shapes and could be used for different purposes. And as God transformed them they became works of art, inspirational and revered. God seems to pick outcasts to glorify him. The less than perfect ones, the ones who were judged, the ones with so much sadness in their lives. He often picks the ones who are different. I realized that all around me at college, there they were: the unloved, broken, and hurt people who didn't fit in. I wanted those people around me to know the love of God waiting for them. As I made more and more of these modern icons of the saints, I realized that my own purpose was not just to make the saints "modern" but to make them look like the people around me, people who reminded me of the saints.

It wasn't hard to imagine the people around me as one of the saints. The saints were all sinful and faced many struggles. Paul the Apostle's life began by killing Christians. Edith Stein, who became Teresa Benedicta of the Cross, was once an atheist.

The Apostle Matthew was a tax collector and traitor to his own people. Augustine of Hippo spent his early life obsessed with success, women, and materialism. Rita of Cascia's family was murderous and violent. Thérèse of Lisieux and Bernadette Soubirous battled illness. The Holy Family lived in poverty. Patrick was a slave. Elizabeth Ann Seton lost her husband and greatest love. Before a change of heart in midlife, Teresa of Ávila had unhealthy friendships and lived a lukewarm life of hostility and gossip in the convent. Francis of Assisi probably struggled to give up his riches; Sebastian his military position. Monica was abused by her husband and had to deal with her rebellious son, Augustine. And Peter, the first pope, betrayed Jesus. When we take away the "saint" prefixes, we more easily see how the saints were like many of the people we know, including ourselves. One day we too can have that prefix in front of our own names.

Since I started creating these paintings (thanks to a heavy dose of the Holy Spirit, I am sure), my non-Christian friends have shown interest in the saints—the *real people*—who looked like them and had similar stories. My work has brought amazing people into my life—people I have met, befriended, and loved. After having known people who felt turned away from Christianity by Christians, I now do all I can to act in *constant* mercy, honesty, and love. Through the way I live, the choices I make, and the way I treat others, I try to love as God loves, unafraid of making mistakes because I know that God loves me more than I could ever imagine.

The more I read the Bible and pray, the more I believe in the power of holiness, and the more I feel enabled to use and spread my gift of creativity. I know this is what God is calling me to do. I used to struggle to share and to integrate these two different parts of my life—my creativity and my faith. But now my gifts have allowed me to share both with others. I now feel free to be wholly myself, which makes my struggles more manageable. I could not have asked for a better gift.

When I use my gifts and see how they affect others, I am reminded that everything should be love—at all costs. It can be so easy for artists to use opportunities, conditions, profits, or networking for their own gain, or for any reason that might be easier or more glamorous. But we must use our gifts for love. Love without condition. Love without questions. Love without ration or reason. Love in the face of betrayal, fear, and misunderstanding. Love unchanging and never lost. Strong love requires sacrifice. It does not change based on the worthiness of the recipient. Loving others the way God loves us changes the way we approach our faith, and it changes how we approach others.

In the diverse lives of the female saints, I also have found a greater love for my identity as a Catholic woman. To be a Catholic woman is to be fearless. To be individual and weird. To be determined and strong. To be radiantly beautiful with a glow of peace and joy. To be unwavering and funny and a wonderful friend. To be both humble and confident. To love at all costs. To be Catholic women is to be who we are, embracing all that makes us each different and special. The more ways we are different, the more ways we can bring God's love to the world and serve him. To be Catholic women means that we are called to support one another and to embrace our similarities and differences. There's a home for all of us in the Church.

Because, the thing is, maybe the Church needs *you* to be the patron saint of scuba diving, or bird-watching, or climate change prevention, or electric guitar playing, or stand-up comedy, or website development. Whatever makes you not quite the same as others is exactly where God might want you to find your purpose. If you really want to share God's love with everyone, you can't be exactly like those around you— the saints show us that. You have your own gifts that give you your own story. I hope someday I'll be painting you and titling it with the prefix "saint."

Peace,

Gracie

GRACIE MORBITZER is a student at the Columbus College of Art and Design in Columbus, Ohio. She enjoys blending urban influences with various aspects of history and culture. Her greatest love is to tell stories with art in many different ways. She hopes to continue painting and telling stories while she pursues a career in museum work or set design. Gracie also plans on traveling a lot, owning a beautiful tiny house, and having a loving, dancing family. She owes everything to her parents, sister, pets, and her wonderful boyfriend. And, of course, above all, she someday hopes to be a saint. You can find her work at themodernsaints.com.

Reflection Question and Prayer

"I used to struggle to share and to integrate these two different parts of my life—my creativity and my faith. But now my gifts have allowed me to share both with others. I now feel free to be wholly myself, which makes my struggles more manageable. I could not have asked for a better gift."

Are there parts of your life that are distant from or untouched by your faith? Brainstorm ways you might be able to unite all of your gifts and interests with your faith. Ask yourself, "How can I use my gifts to serve others in love?"

Pray a Hail Mary for those who have been hurt by Catholics, that they may find healing and a home in the Church. Then, close with this section's petition:

Saint Hildegard, you used your creative and scientific genius in the service of others. Pray that I may use my gifts to give glory to God and to love my neighbor.

"The experience of beauty does not remove us from reality, on the contrary, it leads to a direct encounter with the daily reality of our life, liberating it from darkness, transfiguring it, making it radiant and beautiful."[17]

—Pope Benedict XVI

Protect

Volunteering at a women's shelter

Learning how to compost to care for the environment

Standing up to someone who makes a racist comment

In this section, we'll examine how femininity is expressed through the protection of all God has placed under our care: the innocent, the vulnerable, and all of creation. In these letters, Catholic women reflect on how they have protected life through their various callings.

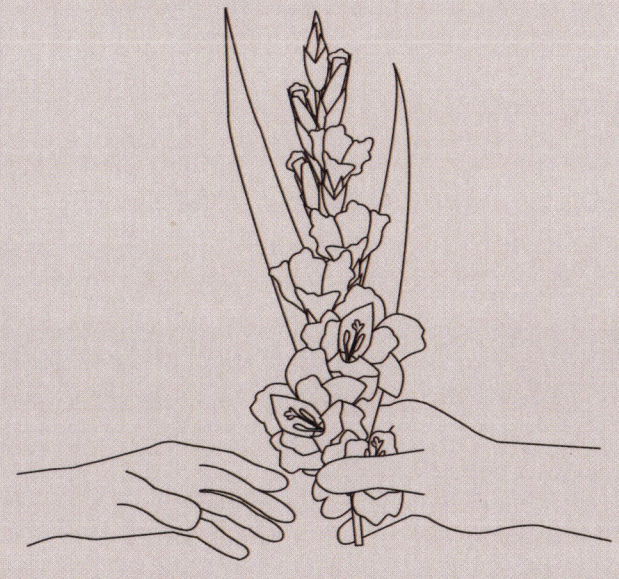

Sister Damien Marie Savino

Sister Damien Marie shares the special places and people that informed her passion for the environment and how she came to realize that the state of the environment is inextricably connected to the state of civilization.

Natalie Alfaro Frazier

Natalie shares how she has come to understand her role as a protector as a Catholic revert and a mother to a daughter with a rare skin condition.

Lauren Costabile

Lauren shares how she was inspired to start a nonprofit to help children with Down syndrome.

Cara Fleury

Cara shares how she and her husband honored the dignity of their unborn child when they became aware that they would likely lose him.

Sister Norma Pimentel

Sister Norma shares how unpredictable moments led her to embrace God's call to stand up for the vulnerable.

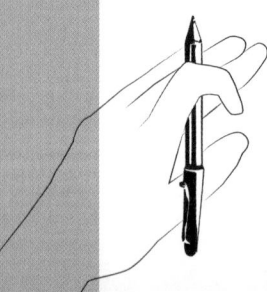

Joan of Arc

Joan of Arc was born to peasant parents in northwestern France in 1412. She had a sound religious upbringing in the Catholic faith and developed a deep love for Jesus and Mary. Around age thirteen, she had a mystical experience in which she heard the voices of Saints Michael the Archangel, Margaret of Antioch, and Catherine of Alexandria. They called her to intensify her faith life and commit herself to the liberation of her people from the English. Just like Mary, the Mother of God, Joan responded with a "yes." She made a vow of virginity and renewed her commitment to the sacraments and prayer.

Four years later, Joan began her mission of liberation. With remarkable strength and determination, she insisted on the veracity of her God-given mission and eventually met with Charles VII, the future king of France. Through gifts of prophecy and vision, Joan managed to persuade the desperate Charles VII to accept her help and went on to win a decisive battle at Orléans. Joan lived with the soldiers she led, evangelizing them with her startling goodness, purity, and courage. A fellow soldier described her behavior thus:

> Except in matters of war, she was simple and innocent. But in the leading and drawing up of armies and in the conduct of war, in disposing an army for battle and haranguing the soldiers, she behaved like the most experienced captain in all the world, like one with a whole lifetime of experience.[22]

Eventually, Joan was taken prisoner by the English and had to endure a long, corrupt trial in which she was accused of witchcraft and condemned as a heretic. She was burned at the stake at age nineteen. She died calling out the name of Jesus.

Saint Joan of Arc is a model of feminine strength and determination as she gave her life for love of Christ and for the protection of her people. In the coming letters, you'll find examples of women who have lived this uniquely feminine strength in various aspects of their lives as well as corresponding quotes, questions, and writing-space for you to prayerfully reflect on how you can live this quality out in your own life.

PRAYER TO SAINT JOAN OF ARC

Saint Joan of Arc, you committed your life to Christ and bravely responded to the call to liberate your people with a resounding "yes." Pray that I may have the courage to always be ready to protect the innocent, the vulnerable, and those God has placed under my care. Amen.

Places of the Heart

Dear Sister in Christ,

Have you ever had a "place of the heart"—a place that you deeply care about and want to protect? A place where you feel a special bond with all that exists and where you awaken to your own humanity and a sense of your place in the world?

One day when I was about seven years old, I was standing in the yard of the house where I grew up in southwestern Connecticut. I was looking toward the trees on the woods' edge. Behind the thick border of trees, hidden out of sight, was a spot beloved to me—a tranquil pond with a willow on its shore, perfect for climbing, and a mystifying island in the middle. My best friend and I spent many hours in that treasured place. We made rafts and found birds' nests on the island, and each year we searched for the great, elusive bullfrog who lived in the surrounding swamp. I proudly identified my first bird there—the red-winged blackbird. I will never forget my childlike excitement at that first primal experience of knowing a creature by name.

On this particular day, while standing there quietly, I knew with a flash of simple insight that I wanted to help nature in some way. I still remember the clarity of my inner thought like it was yesterday. Now, many years later, as a Franciscan Sister of the Eucharist with a doctorate in environmental engineering and degrees in soil science and geography, I can see that this was the first defining moment in my call to protect creation.

That pond was my first place of the heart. There have been many places of the heart since, and each has incrementally deepened and sealed that call. When I was a child, my family spent summer vacations at a cottage colony on a lake in New Hampshire. I loved the lake and all the relationships that went along with it: the friends we saw each year, learning to swim and waterski together, blueberry picking in the mountains, the beauty of sunrises and sunsets on the water, and moments of quiet and peace, especially when the lake was as smooth as glass.

One experience we relished was the freedom of washing our hair in the soft lake water. One year we arrived to signs prohibiting that activity because scientists were concerned that shampoo was polluting the water, adding nutrients that promoted algal growth. I was conflicted by this announcement, both because it meant giving up an enjoyable pastime and because I was saddened by my first hands-on experience of pollution. Yet in having to abstain from washing our hair in the lake from that time on, I learned a valuable life lesson—namely, the importance of sacrificing for a greater good, for the good of a place I loved. I learned that loving the natural world meant not only being captivated by its beauty but also making the personal sacrifices necessary to protect it from harm.

Throughout my teen years, these childhood insights gestated as I became involved in backpacking, cross-country skiing, camping, and the growing Earth Day movement. When I went to college, I planned to major in education. I began to rethink my choice, however, after I took a botany class to fulfill a science requirement. The class so inspired me that I spoke with my parents about this potential change. My father's response was a simple—but life-changing— question: "Where is your heart?" What a defining moment in my call! I went on to major in biogeography at McGill University in Montreal. There I found meaningful friendships with students and faculty whose hearts were equally captivated by the natural world and concerned about its degradation.

At McGill, I was introduced to another place of the heart—the Subarctic. With the encouragement of my professors, I applied to a study abroad program in Finnish Lapland that combined the study of natural and human ecology. Of the twelve students funded, six were science and six anthropology majors. The tundra has a stark beauty all its own, as well as unique environmental challenges because of its fragile nature. And so too, do the native Sami or Lappish peoples. During my time studying abroad, I began to realize the essential links between natural and human communities and the need to protect both. It was another critical step in the unfolding of my call to protect creation.

Pursuing my passion for the subarctic, I stayed on after my study abroad course and traveled to northern Norway, above the Arctic Circle. I was alone, about to graduate from college and searching for direction in life. One night while setting up my tent, I looked up to see the sky alive with dancing, shimmering colors, so vivid and brilliant. It was the northern lights! In the flush of such a stunning moment, the only thing I could think to do was to pull out from my backpack a Bible given to me by a friend in Canada.

At that time, though my parents had brought me up Catholic, I was estranged from the faith and had been since my early teen years. It wasn't science that had pulled me away. In fact, my love of science actually catapulted me on the path back. No, frustration with weak catechesis had convinced me that Catholicism was not relevant to my life. Yet that night beneath the northern lights, as a budding woman-scientist, I knew with irrevocable certainty that there was a God. His footprints were everywhere in his creation. In the face of the grandeur playing out in the sky above, it was clear that he in his goodness had allowed me to be there to experience the beauty of that moment. Even in my smallness and fragility, I was significant in his eyes.

Thus began my reversion to the Catholic faith. I returned to the States, met the Franciscan Sisters of the Eucharist, and discovered that the Lord had impressed a religious calling on my scientific heart. With the encouragement of the Sisters, I completed a Master's degree in soil science and eventually a doctorate in environmental engineering from The Catholic University of America.

My doctoral research led me to another place of the heart—the Anacostia River in Washington, D.C. There, in that neglected, polluted place, I was awakened to what Pope Francis calls "the cry of the earth and the cry of the poor."[29] I began to grasp even more profoundly than I had in Finnish Lapland, the interconnections between natural and human ecology, along with the profound suffering that occurs when those connections are broken. I spent a grace-filled summer interviewing the local residents, learning to see the river through their eyes and not just through scientific reports. Walking along the river with the locals, I saw where they had settled as newly freed slaves, where the herring ran in the spring, and where they baptized by immersion. My heart ached as they recounted how their lives paralleled the degradation of the river—how demoralized they felt when the herring had disappeared and the once-teeming swamps began to fester, when their communities were split by the construction of highways, and when drugs and crime crept in and polluted their place. In coming to know *their* place of the heart, even in its disfigurement, the river became a place of *my* heart, as did its people.

Gradually the Lord guided me to see that I had something special to offer as a woman-engineer. Because of women's unique capacity for relationship and integration, women can soften the hard edge of engineering design and process. We possess the potential, as Saint John Paul II puts it, to put a human face on engineering, to safeguard creation from the inside out, from the heart, as a "service of love."[30] We bring warmth and humanity to situations marred by cold, utilitarian motivations. Women have a natural capacity to live with disordered or "contaminated" situations, to meet ecosystems or people where they are, in the mystery of accompaniment, and to co-suffer with them, as Mary did. Women by nature protect person by person, place by place, by "gestating" a situation or person in relationship, by enwombing and nurturing the organic process of new life.

Through all the "places of the heart" in my life—that now include the beautiful lands of the Franciscan Sisters of the Eucharist, lovingly tended by the sisters—the Lord has taught me how to protect creation as a Catholic woman. And because of the role nature played in my reversion to the faith, I am particularly attuned to the value of ecological experiences for spiritual conversion. In fact, I firmly believe that ecology is an indispensable tool for the New Evangelization.

Dear Sister, I encourage you to find your own places of the heart. Get outside and let nature speak to your heart. Come to know within yourself the profound connection between person and place and cultivate your capacity to safeguard our common home. We read in Scripture that women were the first heralds of the resurrection. Together as Catholic women, let us embrace that role and become heralds of a restored ecology in Christ.

Sincerely, in Christ,
Sister Damien Marie

Go outside and let nature speak to your heart. Come to know within yourself the profound connection between person and place and cultivate your capacity to safeguard our common home. We read in Scripture that women were the first heralds of the resurrection. Together, as Catholic women, let us embrace that role and become heralds of a restored ecology in Christ.

Sister Damien Marie Savino, FSE

SISTER DAMIEN MARIE SAVINO, FSE, PH.D. is a Franciscan Sister of the Eucharist, currently serving as the dean of science and sustainability at Aquinas College in Grand Rapids, Michigan. She has published and lectured widely in scientific and religious circles throughout the United States and abroad. Sister Damien Marie holds a PhD in civil (environmental) engineering and an MA in theology from The Catholic University of America and an MS in soil science from the University of Connecticut. She also earned a BS degree in biogeography from McGill University in Montreal. Her career and religious life have been devoted to interdisciplinary teaching in science and religion, and ecology and theology. In recent years, she has focused on the notion of integral ecology from Pope Francis' encyclical *Laudato Si'*.

Reflection Question and Prayer

"I learned a valuable life lesson—namely, the importance of sacrificing for a greater good, for the good of a place I loved. I learned that loving the natural world meant not only being captivated by its beauty but also making the personal sacrifices necessary to protect it from harm."

Reflect on your relationship with God's creation. How can you practice caring for the Earth, a gift God has given to us?

Say a Hail Mary for guidance to find simple ways to care for the environment, and that every person may come to care for the Earth and protect it from harm. Then, close with this section's petition:

Saint Joan of Arc, you committed your life to Christ and bravely responded to the call to liberate your people with a resounding "yes." Pray that I may have the courage always to be ready to protect the innocent, the vulnerable, and those God has placed under my care. Amen.

Strong, Stubborn Women

Comadre,

When my first child, Oscar, was born, I remember the midwife placing him in front of me on the floor. I was still on my hands and knees surrounded by the familiar environment of my childhood home. Through the darkness of the evening, I was struck with disbelief. I needed a moment to take it all in. As I caught my breath and looked over his little body, I said to him, in my head, "Alright, kid, it's all about to change." I watched my naked, newborn son's body lying in front of me while everyone in the room was watching, waiting for me to scoop him up. In that moment, my understanding of protecting the vulnerable crashed in front of me and finally intertwined with my heart, soul, and brain.

Fast forward two years and this all came to the forefront in a way that I never would have been able to anticipate. My daughter, Olivia, was born eight weeks early with a rare genetic skin condition that we knew nothing about until after I delivered her. I did not feel empowered and strong after her delivery like I did with my son's birth. I was shocked and scared and on the brink of an emotional collapse when the doctors asked if we would like to hold Olivia and say our goodbyes or allow them to try to stabilize her. My brain ping-ponged around. I didn't know the right answer. Again, I found myself with everyone in the room watching me as I caught my breath. But this time I was not on my hands and knees but on a hospital bed while my daughter was being held at the side of a sterile, unknown hospital room. I hadn't even been given the chance to hold her yet. I couldn't really even see her through the white plaques that covered her body. Something stirred in my subconscious. Not waiting until I was sitting to answer, I weakly lifted my arm and breathed, "Help her," trusting it was the Holy Spirit who pushed that answer out of my mouth.

Olivia was transported to a hospital two hours away, and after a short night interrupted by phone calls from doctors and nurses, our family was thrust into three and a half months of hospital living. I was simultaneously trying to protect Oscar from the trauma of feeling pushed aside and uprooted while also trying to protect Olivia from exiting the thin veil between life and death. Every night I dropped into bed from exhaustion, feeling certain I had failed them both only to wake up a few hours later to give it another day. For most of those months while Olivia was in the NICU (newborn intensive care unit), I was running on adrenaline and caffeine. People reminded me each day that my role, as Olivia's mother, was to advocate for her. I was told that I knew her the best because I was her mom. There were times I doubted that, but I just kept showing up because I didn't know what else to do.

Everything that offered stability and normalcy was quickly slipping away. In the subsequent months after Olivia's birth, I ended up losing my job because I couldn't report back to the office. The savings we had from a crowd-sourcing campaign were quickly dwindling. We decided to move halfway across the country, away from everything that felt comforting and normal to me. And yet, our top priority was to maintain routine and normalcy for Oscar and Olivia. It was the only way we knew how to protect them in a world with so little certainty. It has been one long lesson in surrender and trust for me, a lesson I suspect is difficult for all of us but especially so for those who like to feel strong, capable, and independent.

Motherhood was something for which I didn't necessarily long. My mom often talked about how she always knew she wanted to be a mom. I never really gave it much thought until I was on the cusp of marriage. When I was younger, I really struggled to feel comfortable with female stereotypes. I naturally was drawn to strong female characters in history and in books. My personality got me in trouble because I was "too talkative," "bossy," and "too aggressive." I liked feeling strong and fast. I was often put into leadership positions, probably partly in an attempt to steer me on the "right path." But I also think it was because not everyone was like me. Not everyone had the confidence to speak out or stand up for themselves. I didn't mind going toe-to-toe with authority figures if I believed my cause was just. I often took it upon myself to step between people, for better or worse, to try to mediate. I wasn't shy to point out when someone wasn't being very nice. Over the years these characteristics developed into a sense of duty to care for the vulnerable and disenfranchised. It wasn't until my reversion back to the Catholic Church that I connected any of this to motherhood.

Two things solidified my journey back to the Church in college: veneration of Mary and Catholic social teaching. As I tried to figure out my stance on various social issues, I kept finding myself right back at the Catholic Church. Key Catholic figures continuously modeled for me how to respond to my convictions, the things I felt in my gut were right and just. As I studied socioeconomic and geopolitical issues, it increased my conviction that it's our duty as Christians to serve others. I was also learning more about the Church's teachings about the preferential option for the poor, the protection of the most vulnerable in society, and the saints who are venerated for putting their lives on the line to live Catholic social teaching.

It didn't take me long before I stumbled across the way that Mary had been used as a symbol of strength by women's movements in Latin America. She wasn't portrayed as a passive, docile woman. Mary was used to teach about the very uniqueness of womanhood. That carrying life, whether it's spiritual, social, or biological motherhood, is what sets women apart. It's hard to deny that motherhood in and of itself is radical hospitality and offering service and love to the most vulnerable among us. The Church plainly values the strength and uniqueness that only women can offer the world. Mary's life is celebrated throughout the liturgical calendar to highlight her femininity, her strength, and her essential role in our salvation. For the first time, I saw Mary as a woman worth modeling myself after and that was enough for me to know that my Protestant feminist peers were really missing out on one of their strongest allies: Our Lady, the Mother of God. Mary's role both as a life-giving and a grieving mother transformed my understanding of womanhood.

As Catholics, we want to protect the innocent, the vulnerable, and the marginalized. We hear about it almost every Sunday. We are reminded of the hospitality, the forgiveness, and the love that our God-fearing ancestors exhibited time and time again. Our Holy Mother, Mary, painstakingly models for us the innate desire that mothers have to protect their children and the gritty reality that there's only so much protecting that can be done in the face of the fallen world. It was hard for me to fathom Mary's sorrow before having children. Really, it was hard for me to fathom it until my husband and I were told that we might lose Olivia. At the foot of the cross, Mary surrendered to God's will and trusted in his goodness. Because of Mary's determination as a mother and her strength as a woman, she is not only hated by Satan but feared by Satan. Mary showed me that the Church needs strong stubborn women like her. Like so many of the saints. Like me. Like you. Mary, Mother of God, pray for us.

In solidarity,

Natalie

At the foot of the cross, Mary surrendered to God's will and trusted in his goodness. Because of Mary's determination as a mother and her strength as a woman, she is not only hated by Satan but feared by Satan. Mary showed me that the Church needs strong stubborn women like her. Like so many of the saints. Like me. Like you. Mary, Mother of God, pray for us.

Natalie

NATALIE ALFARO FRAZIER grew up in California's Central Coast region in a Catholic Nicaraguan-American family. While studying global development studies at Seattle Pacific University, she had a reversion to the faith. Natalie later returned to California and received her master's in public administration from Middlebury Institute of International Studies at Monterey. Natalie is passionate about community-driven social change and radical hospitality. One of her favorite things to do is drink a good cup of coffee and have a good conversation while walking along the beach. Natalie now lives in the Nashville area with her husband, two children, and another one on the way. You can read more about her family's journey after her daughter, Olivia, was born with Harlequin Ichthyosis, a rare genetic skin condition, at coyotesandsaints.com.

Reflection Question and Prayer

"People reminded me each day that my role, as Olivia's mother, was to advocate for her. I was told that I knew her the best because I was her mom. There were times I doubted that, but I just kept showing up because I didn't know what else to do."

For whom has God called you to be an advocate? Reflect and pray about actions you can take today to care for the vulnerable, poor, and innocent. Then, pray a Hail Mary for women in the Church and close with this section's petition:

Saint Joan of Arc, you committed your life to Christ, evangelization, and prayer, and you responded to the call to liberate your people with a resounding "yes." Pray that I may have the courage to always be ready to protect the innocent, the vulnerable, and all of the creation that God has placed under our care. Amen.

If we have no peace, it is because we have forgotten that we belong to each other."[27]

—Mother Teresa

Protecting
the Vulnerable

Dear Sisters in Christ,

God has written a beautiful story for each of our lives. And I believe God created me with the vocation to love by serving those with Down syndrome. I have met and delighted in many of these unique souls—who just happen to be rocking an extra chromosome!

My first encounter with someone with Down syndrome happened when I was eighteen years old. I spent a week of my summer volunteering as a camp counselor for children with disabilities. My older brother had been volunteering at the camp since he was sixteen. He had always asked me to volunteer with him. He would tell me how amazing it was, but every year I would decide at the last minute that I didn't want to go. I don't know if I declined out of fear or selfishness or a little of both. But, at that point in my life, I couldn't imagine doing much for someone else, let alone taking care of someone with a disability. I was your typical high school senior, self-centered and worried about the opinions of others. Basically, my priorities were all out of whack.

After years of saying "no" to my brother, for some reason after I graduated from high school I said "yes." Perhaps it was because I was going to college so I wanted a new beginning, a fresh start. I was determined to challenge myself to do more for others. Looking back, I can see it was all part of God's perfect plan. He has a beautiful way of bringing all things together for our good at just the right time (see Rom 8:28). Prior to the camp, I had not interacted much with people with special needs, and I had never really known anyone with Down syndrome.

On the first day of camp, all the counselors and campers gathered together in the rec hall. The campers were between fifteen and twenty-five years old, and most of them were taller and bigger than me. To be honest, I felt very intimidated and inadequate. Campers were all over the place. Some were running around yelling, others were jumping, and some were even crying. I felt so overwhelmed by the noise that I retreated inward and just awkwardly stood alone. I didn't know how to relate or act around the campers. As I looked across the room, I made eye contact with a boy with Down syndrome who had seen me standing by myself. He smiled at me, and I smiled back. Before I knew it, he was running over to me. He put his arms around me and gave me the biggest bear hug. It was the sweetest thing ever!

Have you ever received a hug from someone with Down syndrome? Let me tell you, it's like receiving a hug from Jesus himself! The heart of a child with Down syndrome is a glimpse into heaven. The joy and love they exude is infectious. The boy then introduced himself to me and we bonded over the fact that we were both first timers. He had instantly broken down my walls and made me feel more comfortable. He sensed that I needed a friend, and through a simple gesture he showed me joy and love. This boy's hug will remain with me forever. It was the first time God opened my eyes to see into the hearts of those with Down syndrome.

I see the face of God in every person I meet with Down syndrome, but it's particularly true with my friend Judy. She is one of the most beautiful people I've ever known. We've been friends for about five years now, and from the moment I met Judy, I knew she was something special. Her spirit is so joyful, it's contagious. I call her my "hype woman" because she's constantly complimenting and building up those around her. She makes her family and friends, including me, feel so loved! She's always the life of the party. Judy's an amazing dancer, super confident, so funny, and incredibly charismatic. Whether we're going out to dinner, attending a concert or a baseball game, or just singing

Sacred Scripture continually speaks to us of an active commitment to our neighbor and demands of us a shared responsibility for all of humanity. This duty is not limited to one's own family, nation or state, but extends progressively to all . . . so no one can consider himself extraneous or indifferent to the lot of another member of the human family."[26]

—Saint John Paul II

karaoke and dancing all night, without fail she always says, "Today was the best day ever!" And she genuinely means it. Of course, just like anyone else, Judy has bad days. But she's able to look beyond her bad days and focus on the good. Her positive outlook inspires me to look at the world in the same way, with eyes of joy and simple gratitude. Judy is a living example of God's infinite love manifested in the human person, and she has brought indescribable joy to me and to everyone she encounters. I'm forever grateful to call her my friend.

The more time I spend with those with Down syndrome, the more God reveals to me that I am on this earth to serve them. One summer, after visiting Uganda, East Africa, I felt convinced that the Lord was calling me to be a voice for the voiceless and to fight for children with Down syndrome who can't always fight for themselves. What I had seen in Uganda really saddened me; children with Down syndrome typically are seen as a burden to society. Due to poverty and lack of education and resources, children with Down syndrome also often don't have access to the most basic medical care. According to the National Down Syndrome Society, "approximately half of all infants born with Down syndrome have a heart defect that requires surgery to repair." Families in Uganda and other developing countries, however, often don't have the funds or access to receive the open-heart surgery, so as a result, many children with Down syndrome are dying.

After I returned home, I couldn't shake what I had seen and experienced. My friend Judy had been born with a heart defect, but she was able to get it corrected here in the United States with surgery. Now she's thriving in her young adult life. Meanwhile, many children with Down syndrome born in developing countries are not given the same opportunity. I began to pray about what God wanted me to do with what I had experienced, and I felt him asking me to help. So, I created a nonprofit called Hearts of Joy International that provides lifesaving heart surgery for children with Down syndrome in countries where families can't afford medical care. We currently serve children in India, Uganda, and the Philippines.

Whether physical or spiritual, all women are called to motherhood. Our role is to protect, guide, love, and nurture. I feel deeply called to serve the most vulnerable, those society deems as having no value, because I see their tremendous purpose and

The more time I spend with those with down syndrome, the more God reveals to me that I am on this earth to serve them.
— Lauren Costabile

value in the eyes of God. I have discovered my spiritual motherhood in caring for children with Down syndrome. I fight for their chance to receive proper medical care, educate and empower their families, and nurture a culture of life.

We all have a purpose to fulfill, a way God desires us to love in the world. All we have to do is say "yes" to his plans for us! Yet, often we get overwhelmed and start to believe lies that we're not good enough or capable of the great things to which God calls us. But God will never ask us to do something we cannot do. We may think we're not capable, but God sees beyond our human capacities. He sees our full potential and our truest capabilities. He sees us more clearly than we can see ourselves. If something is truly his will, he will give us the grace and strength to do it.

Sisters, God has given each of you a unique mission and purpose that only you can fulfill. God has engraved in your hearts a unique vocation to love. Each woman's vocation to love will look different, but that's the beauty of it. Don't be afraid to step out and say "yes" to what God is asking of you. Be courageous! Take a leap of faith and trust that God will catch you, because *he will*. He has amazing plans for each one of us. Will it be scary? Yes. Will it be challenging? Yes. But will it be worth it? Absolutely.

I'm constantly humbled by God's unique call in my life. Following God's will has been the most challenging thing I've ever done, and it continues to stretch my heart in unimaginable ways. My patience is tested, and my trust in the Lord sometimes wears thin. But I also wouldn't change this call for anything in the world. I have such peace and joy knowing that I'm living out the vocation to which God has called me—I've never felt so alive. Sisters, God wants this for each one of us. He created us with such perfect attention to detail, each with unique missions, gifts, and talents. So, if God is asking something of you—SAY YES—even if it's unknown or unfamiliar. God doesn't make mistakes. He will send you right where he wants you to be. He will equip you with all you need for the awesome mission he has written on your heart. It may not be easy, but he will bless you abundantly for your faith and obedience.

Saint John Paul II once proclaimed, "Life with Christ is a wonderful adventure."[31] Let's get ready for the greatest adventure of our lives!

United in prayer,

Lauren

Lauren Costabile is a Catholic speaker, advocate for those with Down syndrome, and founder of Hearts of Joy International (heartsofjoyinternational.com). A New Jersey native, she loves all things gluten free, and she strives to use her gifts and talents to spread joy and to make our world a brighter place.

Reflection Question and Prayer

"Our role is to protect, guide, love, and nurture. I feel deeply called to serve the most vulnerable, those society deems as having no value, because I see their tremendous purpose and value in the eyes of God. I have discovered my spiritual motherhood in caring for children with Down syndrome. I fight for their chance to receive proper medical care, educate and empower their families, and nurture a culture of life."

Within your own life, how can you build a "culture of life"? In what ways can you better practice respect for the dignity of every human person?

Say a Hail Mary for those with Down syndrome and for the building up of a culture of life. Then, close with this section's petition:

Saint Joan of Arc, you committed your life to Christ and bravely responded to the call to liberate your people with a resounding "yes." Pray that I may have the courage to always be ready to protect the innocent, the vulnerable, and those God has placed under my care. Amen.

A Fierce Love

Dear Sister in Christ,

Nothing in life is certain. No amount of planning, organizing, preparing, or dreaming will guarantee a desired outcome. I'm constantly reminded to loosen my grip and to let Jesus take over.

A few years ago, my husband's father passed away from cancer, and just one month later, we found out that we were expecting another child. The joy was palpable—a life given just as a life had been taken. In the midst of our grief, God gave us hope. I giggled as I imagined how much busier our life soon would become. Another baby joining our family of five. After that moment of daydreaming, I then wasted no time making plans. Within twenty-four hours of the positive pregnancy test, I had already calculated my due date, how many years apart the children would be in school (including college), and planned where the new baby would sleep. I realized that the baby's arrival would be amid a busy schedule of baseball practices and summer vacation. I had a tight grip on a life that wasn't mine alone to steer. As it turned out, no amount of planning could prepare me for the news that came twelve weeks later.

As we anxiously awaited a call from the doctor regarding the gender of our baby, I made plans for a gender reveal cake, a surprise for our kids that weekend. I got lost in daydreams about what my children's reactions might be to either a blue or pink cake and couldn't wait to find out which storyline would play out. The phone rang, and I could almost hear the drumroll. Then I heard words I had never expected, "Unfortunately, the test results were positive for Trisomy 13." My heart raced, and I stared at my husband. I felt paralyzed. I didn't know what to say or what to ask. What did this mean? Plans on hold. Preparations rerouted. We soon found out that Trisomy 13 is a chromosomal defect described by medical literature as "incompatible with life." Most babies with the disorder do not make it to full term, and those that do often only live for hours, days, or one year. I wondered, *What of our many dreams for this child? What of those, Lord?*

"The most deadly poison of our times is indifference . . . And this happens, although the praise of God should know no limits. Let us strive, therefore, to praise him to the greatest extent of our powers."[24]

—Saint Maximilian Kolbe

Weeks before that call, in my organizational frenzy, I had started making lists of possible names for the baby. I hadn't paid much attention to girls' names because I had been almost sure our baby was a boy. So, when I received the news, I asked the gender of the baby. *Boy.* The next day, we decided to name our son. We couldn't allow him to remain a question mark. We named him Beau Gabriel Fleury; Beau means "handsome," and Gabriel means "messenger of the Lord." These names encompassed everything we knew to be true about our little boy. With this naming came the gift of freedom and total acceptance; it was our *fiat.* No longer bound by fear and confusion, I was moved by a deep love to fiercely protect this child. My son, Beau Gabriel, was helping me to walk the road of holiness, a role reversal I never had seen coming.

Later that week, an ultrasound confirmed that the development of Beau's arms, legs, and brain were consistent with the initial test. We were devastated. We had watched him bounce around on the screen with such great hope! I kept searching for a way out, for a different end to the story, but the Lord kept asking me to trust him. My husband and I sat in silence as the implications of the Trisomy 13 diagnosis were explained to us. The doctor discussed our "options" (including abortion), but there was no decision to be made. How could we say "no" to the Lord when he is the reason for our many blessings? A "no" to God was an impossibility for us because a "no" to him for one thing would also mean a "no" to his many gifts of love in our lives. We trusted that God would work through our pain to bring peace and healing to others. Beau was a little missionary, and his work was just beginning.

The Lord asked me a very specific question that day: "Will you love this child as I have loved you?" This question, like a dagger to the heart, immediately brought to mind the countless times in my life that I had denied Christ. He was asking me, "Cara, will you love this child in all of his imperfections? Will you love him fully despite the brevity of his life?" In that moment, I realized that the Lord was calling me to unconditional love, much like his love for me, in all of my imperfections. My "yes" to motherhood took on a new meaning through Beau. It was a "yes" to self-denial and a promise to nurture and protect. It was a "no" to self-reliance and control. It was a "yes" to heartache, but also a powerful "yes" to love.

That night, overcome with exhaustion and emotion, my husband and I collapsed on our bedroom floor and bawled. Knowing that we were embracing a child's life with an imminent end brought on a very raw sorrow and a profoundly intimate moment in our marriage. We embraced this intense and all-encompassing suffering because we so deeply loved this little boy who we knew we might never get to hold. The grief was overwhelming. Falling in love always entails a risk of heartbreak, and as parents, we often take for granted that being open to life makes us vulnerable to another kind of heartache and loss. Being open to life is to be open to death.

Though I accepted God's will for our family and this child, I fervently prayed for the chance to hold him. Even if only for a few hours, I wanted to hold my son. As per usual, I also started making plans. We shared the news with family and close friends in a letter. I then began to consider what life might look like if Beau had an extended stay in the hospital after delivery or if we ended up needing in-home nursing care once he came home.

One afternoon, as I sat in the parking lot of my son's school, I decided to write Beau a letter:

> You are not an unfortunate event or random spasm of chromosomes. You were destined by God from the beginning of time for this life, just as you are. There were no mistakes or coincidences when God gently knit you in my womb. The perfect artist created you in his infinite wisdom and loving masterful hands. He gifted you to us, your mother and father, as a masterpiece of his love and perfect design. You are a beauty unto yourself and an awe-inspiring wonder of life. You are our source of love, and we are humbled to be yours. You, my sweet son, are so loved. For everything you are and for every breath you ever take, you are our greatest privilege and most cherished joy.

Two weeks after Beau's diagnosis was confirmed, I was rushed to the emergency room with severe bleeding. After being told to wait in line like everyone else, I spent three hours in the waiting room. My heart ached beyond words for the son I felt

As I lay in the hospital bed at 2 a.m., writhing in pain from contractions that continued for hours, I united my suffering to Christ: his physical pain, vulnerability, the mockery and shame, and faith in God's will. It was in my poverty that I understood sacrificial love.

Cara Fleming

powerless to protect. Suddenly, the room started to spin. I lost my vision, and my blood pressure plummeted. Twelve hours of every kind of pain one could imagine followed: physical, mental, emotional, and spiritual. During those twelve hours, I identified with Our Lady's suffering more intimately than ever before and accompanied her to the foot of the cross. There, I found comfort and an opportunity to offer up my sadness. Under Our Lady's mantle, I found refuge and understanding. But it wasn't until the physical pain of the violent delivery that I identified most closely with Christ and his Cross. As I lay in the hospital bed at 2 a.m., writhing in pain from contractions that continued for hours, I united my suffering to Christ: his physical pain, vulnerability, the mockery and shame, and faith in God's will. It was in my poverty that I understood sacrificial love.

God called Beau to heaven that night.

Healing has been a long road, but the Lord has never abandoned us. The process of naming, celebrating, and burying Beau has been instrumental in healing after this tragedy. Though I never got the chance to hold Beau this side of heaven, I am at peace knowing he is fully alive in heaven, surrounded by loved ones who have gone before us and in the arms of Jesus and Mary. We trust that our first hugs with Beau will be the sweetest imaginable.

Dear sisters, we can be tempted to mistake our vocational fulfillment for social-media-worthy achievements, or a "superwoman" drive for success, or a finished to-do list. But true peace is only found in the fulfillment of a higher calling to love others before ourselves. Look for opportunities in your day-to-day life to love and nurture those around you. We bring Christ to others through the simplest acts of kindness, generosity, and compassion. Perhaps it's a cheerful smile shared with a stranger or time given to a friend in need. In making ourselves smaller, Christ becomes bigger. Let his light shine through you, even when you are struggling. Be consoled knowing that the Lord moves in our hearts in moments of joy as well as in moments of great sadness. He calls each of us to walk a specific path to holiness. He uses our vulnerability to teach us, to humble us, and to bring hope to others through our stories. We are all called to love, to serve, and to witness. In this call to nurture others, we can find fulfillment, joy, and peace. So love boldly and fiercely, keeping your gaze on the Lord at all times!

In Jesus,
Cara

CARA FLEURY has always been that girl with a cheerful smile, a kind heart, and a bounce in her step. After graduating from Georgetown University, Cara pursued a professional dance career in musical theatre in New York City. She then returned to the Washington, D.C., area to work as a choreographer and history teacher for two all-girl Catholic high schools. She now lives in northern Virginia in a laughter-filled home with her husband Al and four children. She draws great inspiration from the gift of faith and the freedom to celebrate it joyfully. Still a dreamer and an artist at heart, Cara's joy shines through her writing, recipe creations, baking adventures, and epic dance parties thrown in the family room with her favorite five people in the world. Cara is behind Brave Marshmallow, a blog that inspires families to live and love wholeheartedly through stories, letters to children.

Reflection Question and Prayer

"Dear sisters, we can be tempted to mistake our vocational fulfillment for social-media-worthy achievements, or a 'superwoman' drive for success, or a finished to-do list. But true peace is only found in the fulfillment of a higher calling to love others before ourselves. Look for opportunities in your day-to-day life to love and nurture those around you."

What are some little ways you love the people around you already? When do you struggle to love them? Close your eyes and imagine yourself in those difficult moments. Ask God what you could do differently to better love the people in front of you.

Pray a Hail Mary for women and families who have lost children and for the lives of the unborn. Then, close with this section's petition:

Saint Joan of Arc, you committed your life to Christ and bravely responded to the call to liberate your people with a resounding "yes." Pray that I may have the courage to always be ready to protect the innocent, the vulnerable, and those God has placed under my care. Amen.

do not be afraid to say "yes" to God in those unpredictable moments that happen by chiripa. These moments may help define who you are and direct the path before you.

Sister Norma

Standing for Others

Dear Sister,

A series of *chiripas*, or mere chances, brought me to where I am today. It all started when my father crossed into the United States to find out what he needed to do to move his family to the country. He filled out the application and was told he had to stay in the United States until he got a response. My mother was pregnant with me at the time, and as a result, I was born in the United States and not in Mexico—by *chiripa*.

My father's American dream led my life to begin in the United States, ultimately establishing the route by which I would discover who I would become. As I grew up, coming and going between two countries, the United States and Mexico, I came to appreciate two cultures. This gave me a special sensitivity for the other. Because of my upbringing, I deeply understood that someone different from me could be a part of who I was at the same time.

After I graduated from college, God somehow got a hold of me. Up until then I had been entirely focused on myself. I was excited about my professional career and the possibilities it would bring. I knew my passion and curiosity for life would lead me to something special—but I never expected what came next. By *chiripa*, I ended up at a prayer group one evening. At the time, I was only there because I was interested in going out with my friends for pizza afterward, and I had to tag along in order to get a ride. It turns out God had other plans. I was completely mesmerized by the encounter with God that I experienced in prayer that night. It was as if scales fell from my eyes, and I began seeing all of life through a different lens.

I was swept off my feet by our amazing Lord and Savior. As a result, I "eloped" with him and chose to enter religious life with the Missionaries of Jesus. The day I left for the convent, I didn't even tell my parents. I had to come back the next day to let them know what I'd done. In the convent, I came to discover myself more directly in relationship with God. Through the Missionaries of Jesus' daily community life, I was introduced to many immigrant families. In the early days of my novitiate, the

Border Patrol would call our convent to see if we could take in immigrant families because they didn't have a detention facility. Immigrant mothers and their children were always a part of our community life at the convent.

Later, Bishop John J. Fitzpatrick asked my religious order to oversee the refugee shelter Casa Oscar Romero. There, we helped tens of thousands of immigrants in the 1980s. During the time I was working in Casa Oscar Romero, I came to know more personally the struggles and suffering of refugees arriving in the United States. Daily we would hear stories of the atrocities they experienced back home and as they journeyed to our country. I came to understand the importance of what we were doing to help restore the refugees' dignity.

While at Casa Oscar Romero, also I learned an important lesson that helped define who I am today. On our way to lunch one day, Sister Juliana Garcia (who oversaw the day-to-day operations at the Casa), asked me to go with her to show support for a group that would be demonstrating at the local congressman's office. The group was speaking in defense of the people we helped every day at the refugee shelter. Soon after we arrived, however, the police arrived and began arresting everyone. Sister Juliana turned to me and said, "Norma, when you believe in something but you run away when things get tough, then you don't stand for anything. *No eres nadie* ('You are no one')."

As Sister Juliana spoke, I was bewildered by all that was happening. I watched in disbelief as police dragged people off in handcuffs. But as I listened to Sister Juliana tell me how we needed to stand firm and support the group because they were standing up for people's lives, I felt empowered to acknowledge my stance no matter what was about to unfold. I had never done anything to break the law. But today I was going to be arrested! At one point, Sister Juliana looked at me and said, "We both can't get arrested. Someone has to take care of the shelter. So, you decide." I looked at her, and I remember thinking to myself that I was the younger one (I was twenty five at the time), so I replied, "I guess it's me." She nodded in agreement and said, "Okay, bye." And then she left!

As Sister Juliana walked away, I suddenly felt alone. The sense of strength, wisdom, and confidence she had given me while standing at my side left with her, and I had to find those things within me. As scared as I was in that moment, I decided to wait to be arrested and placed in handcuffs. But first I found my way to the back of the room to give myself some extra time to be ready for the inevitable. When my turn came to be arrested, I offered my hands up to be handcuffed and immediately told the officer, "I will walk." I couldn't see myself being dragged away by force. As I walked to the police car, a cameraman from the local news station shouted from the crowd, "Sister, you're here also?" I responded with words that have continued to echo throughout my life, "Yes. And you should be here as well. Everyone who believes in defending life should be here."

As funny as it sounds, Sister Juliana's abrupt departure was a decisive moment in my life. It defined who I am, what I stand for, and how much I'm willing to do for others. Because of moments like these, I came to know that God calls me to defend and protect the poor, the vulnerable—all those who need us to defend human life. We all have these defining moments in life. But sometimes we are more caught up with the trends of the day. Perhaps we are more interested in owning an expensive pair of shoes or a piece of new technology that costs more than some people make in a month. I pray, however, that someday all of us may realize that those things are unimportant on the journey to discover God's plan for our lives.

The Lord has blessed you with unique gifts and talents to do his work. I urge you to recognize them. Put them to use. As women in the Church, we have a unique calling to be present to those among us. We can learn from so many outstanding women. I'm grateful, for example, that I had the privilege of learning from Sister Juliana. I also continue to draw inspiration from other religious sisters and laywomen with whom I work every day. I encourage you to seek out good mentors. Don't forget about the saints. We have some excellent role models in the saints, beginning with our Blessed Mother Mary.

Some people tell me that I am like "the calm in the storm." If I am, it's only because prayer guides every step I take. My prayer life is key for who I am today and what I do. If I didn't make the time to wake up early in the morning, go to Mass and pray, and then end the night with prayers, I think I would get lost in all the day's demands. Remember always, Jesus Christ himself is guiding us to care for his people. As Catholic women, we are called to pass that message on to everyone who needs to hear it, by our actions and with our words.

Oftentimes in my work I find myself in a room full of men. I've been the only woman in a room full of law enforcement agents and city leaders meeting to discuss plans to address the humanitarian crisis occurring along our border. As the only woman, I want to think that my voice and my presence helped them to remember to be compassionate in their plans and strategies. As women, we don't have to speak the loudest. We don't have to command all the attention in a room. But we do have to say what needs to be said. Most importantly, we need to be women of action.

If you want change in your community, go out and get to work. Learn to swim against the current of a culture that focuses too much on the "isms" of individualism, consumerism, and materialism. I'm not saying it will be easy, but I promise you it will be worth it. Above all, do not be afraid to say "yes" to God in those unpredictable moments that happen by *chiripa*. These moments may help define who you are and direct the path before you. As you look for ways to make a difference in the world, I pray that God will shine his light and give you a *buen camino*.

Wishing you grace and blessings on your path,
Sister Norma Pimentel

SISTER NORMA PIMENTEL, MJ, was born and raised in Brownsville, Texas, and entered the Missionaries of Jesus when she was twenty-two years old. As executive director of Catholic Charities of the Rio Grande Valley in south Texas, she organizes community resources to help Central Americans seeking asylum in the United States. In response to recent surges of refugees, she founded the Humanitarian Respite Center at Sacred Heart Church in McAllen, Texas. Recently, in a special moment via satellite broadcast to Sacred Heart Church, Pope Francis recognized Sister Norma for her work and thanked her for her humility and encouraged her to continue her efforts to help immigrants.

Reflection Question and Prayer

"At one point, Sister Juliana looked at me and said, 'We both can't get arrested. Someone has to take care of the shelter. So, you decide.' I looked at her, and I remember thinking to myself that I was the younger one (I was twenty five at the time), so I replied, 'I guess it's me.' . . . As funny as it sounds, Sister Juliana's abrupt departure was a decisive moment in my life. It defined who I am, what I stand for, and how much I'm willing to do for others. Because of moments like these, I came to know that God calls me to defend and protect the poor, the vulnerable—all those who need us to defend human life."

In what aspects of your life can you stand for others and protect their dignity? Pray a Hail Mary for growth in courage and for the protection of immigrants and refugees, especially families. Then, close with this section's petition:

Saint Joan of Arc, you committed your life to Christ, evangelization, and prayer, and you responded to the call to liberate your people with a resounding "yes." Pray that I may have the courage to always be ready to protect the innocent, the vulnerable, and all of the creation that God has placed under our care. Amen.

Lead

Responding to an unmet need in your community

Meeting a young person seeking guidance for coffee

Walking the road less traveled

In this section, we'll examine how femininity is expressed through identifying a need and responding to it through various forms of leadership. In these letters, Catholic women reflect on the diverse ways they have embraced leadership and been trailblazers in their unique circumstances.

Shanel Adams

Shanel shares how a novena to Saint Thérèse of Lisieux helped her to embrace the direction of God's will in her life.

Katie Waldow

Katie shares her journey with infertility and how it has led her to care for and walk with other women who have experienced it too.

Lisa Brenninkmeyer

Lisa gives an honest, vulnerable account of the difficulties that come with leadership and the importance of forming friendships.

Sarah Kroger

Sarah shares how she found the courage and humility necessary to embrace her creative gifts and give glory to God.

Eve Tushnet

Eve shares how she has found a path in the Church amid seemingly irreconcilable elements of her life and how you can too.

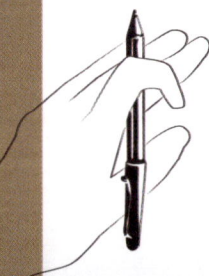

Patron Saint

Catherine of Siena

Catherine Benincasa, born on March 25, 1347, was one of twenty-five children of wealthy parents who ran a cloth-dying business in Siena, Italy. As a child, she made a vow of virginity and committed herself to a life of prayer and works of charity for the sick and suffering. She later entered the Third Order of Dominicans as a layperson, which allowed her to live quietly from home with her family. She frequently gave away her family's food and clothing to those in need. When there was an outbreak of the plague, she spent her time with the suffering. A priest who had known her since her childhood observed that she was never more admirable than at this time: "She was constantly near those who were attacked by the epidemic; she prepared them for death and buried them with her own hands."[32]

As Catherine's reputation for holiness grew, she was sought after for spiritual guidance from many different leaders. She became a mentor to many and would come to be called "mother." She saw herself as guiding each of her spiritual children. Catherine also traveled across Europe to foster peace and press for the internal reform of the Church.[33] At that time in history, the papacy had moved out of Rome to Avignon, France, and as a result, was

> "The Church receives great benefit from the exercise of spiritual motherhood by so many women, lay and consecrated, who nourish souls with thoughts of God, who strengthen the people's faith and direct Christian life towards ever loftier peaks."[34]
>
> —Pope Benedict XVI

becoming increasingly influenced by French politics and lifestyle, that were largely corrupt. Catherine wrote fifteen letters to Pope Gregory XI, urging him to listen to the Holy Spirit and return to Rome. He eventually relented and returned to Rome, largely due to Catherine's witness. After falling ill, Catherine died in Rome when she was only thirty-three. She was canonized in 1461 and named a Doctor of the Church in 1970.

Saint Catherine of Siena is a model of a firm and daring feminine leader. Her life was an example of humble leadership concerned only with serving Christ and others. In the coming letters, you'll find examples of women who have embraced various forms of leadership in their lives as well as corresponding quotes, questions, and writing-space for you to prayerfully reflect on how you can live this quality out in your own life.

PRAYER TO
SAINT CATHERINE OF SIENA

Saint Catherine of Siena, you devoted yourself to the sick, the suffering, and the spiritually needy. You also mediated disputes, brokered peace between warring factions, and provided guidance to popes and political leaders. Pray that if I am called to lead that I might do so in humility and with a spirit of Christ-like service to those in need. Amen.

"History is written almost exclusively as the narrative of men's achievements, when in fact its better part is most often molded by women's determined and persevering action for good. . . . How much still needs to be said and written about man's enormous debt to woman in every other realm of social and cultural pro-gress! The Church and human society have been, and continue to be, measurelessly enriched by the unique presence and gifts of women, especially those who have consecrated themselves to the Lord and in him have given themselves in service to others."[36]

—Saint John Paul II

Little Roses of Leadership

Dear Sister,

When I joined the Catholic Church, I thought I knew all of the reasons I was there. I had testimonies of beautiful experiences tucked in my pocket to share. I reveled in the idea of being more contemplative, more reverent. I loved lighting candles and kneeling during Mass. I felt moved by the intelligibility of my priest's homilies. And there was nothing more inviting than the soft mysticism of women—old and young, black and white—who quickly became friends. This twenty-something, overworked, young professional was in love. But like most love stories, I had no idea what I was getting myself into.

Looking back, I was so naïve. My theological understanding was lacking. I had no clue there were so many differences between the Catholic faith and my Baptist up-bringing. For instance, the intercession of the saints. Like most converts, this aspect of the faith gave me long pause. It was my "*I like everything else, but I don't know about this*" part. Luckily, my mother was joining the Church also, and she was all in. Every time something made me fearful, she jokingly called me an "overthinker" or broke down a massive apologetics issue into three simple words, "It feels right." I decided to trust her and all the Catholics with strong faith who had embraced me.

Well into the RCIA process, my relationship with the saints was still reluctant. Saint Thérèse of Lisieux was the saint who eventually pushed me out of my quiet suspicion. She came out of nowhere. I was randomly looking for prayers online while at work, and a novena for her intercession stood out to me. I did not know anything about her. I didn't even know what a novena was! Nevertheless, there I was praying for her intercession in an office cubicle at my corporate communications job. I needed a sign from God *bad*.

My prayer intention was to ask where I should take my career next. I'd wanted to be a writer for as long as I can remember, but writing emails for an automotive company wasn't what I had envisioned. My love for books had led me to begin studying for a master's in library science, but I wasn't sure I was meant to do that either. At the same time, Progressionista, the small book club program I started for preteen girls in my neighborhood, was growing into an established nonprofit. As much as I loved the mission of Progressionista—exposing Detroit girls to phenomenal career women and gifting them exciting new reads each month—the idea of leading a nonprofit didn't feel right. I wanted to be an artist and a servant, but it felt like people were praising me for being a woman with a brand and a title. I found myself resenting the attention it brought me. After I prayed for Saint Thérèse's intercession, I was constantly looking out for a grand moment when I would receive a sign. I had read so many stories of people receiving roses as signs of her intercession; I imagined being handed a rose as a sign that I was meant to write the next big American novel. I thought I would hear Thérèse's name come up during a moment that clarified that I needed to leave my job immediately and run off to the other side of the world to write. Funnily, it was as though all the roses in the world had dried up during my novena. I never saw one or perceived any sign that pointed to her intercession. After a while, I forgot about my prayer, and I no longer looked for a sign. I figured it had been ridiculous to expect one and continued to dive into my new Catholic faith in other ways that deepened my longing to find God's true path for me. Without much choice, I began to embrace Progressionista's growth little by little. More girls wanted to be a part of the book club, and it pushed me to do something about it. I wrote and received a grant to open another chapter of the book club on Detroit's eastside. I also expanded the nonprofit by partnering with a friend to start a Progressionista chapter in her hometown of Chicago. Within a year, the organization's impact had tripled. I found an incomparable peace as I witnessed more and more girls light up when they would meet diverse career women, do hands-on activities with each other, and grab their brand-new books to take home. With fear still resting in my chest, I prayed for courage before and after every step I made. I started spiritual direction and was open about all of my fears about letting Progressionista grow. I was honest and vulnerable every session, allowing myself to navigate my feelings that my career had not gone the way I had intended. I admitted that I was overwhelmed. The graces I received from these sessions were life transforming and made me realize that Progressionista did not have to be my undertaking—it could be God's, if I just could trust him more.

When I finally began to embrace my call to be a leader of Progressionista, I realized that Saint Thérèse already had sent me a sign. I had given a girl at my church some leftover books from the book club. Her father was over-the-moon appreciative and thanked me for weeks. I was overwhelmed by his gratitude; that's just how much he stressed his appreciation. One time, while I was at a women's retreat, my mother said he had come to Mass with one last thank-you for me. She told me he had handed her a flower. I brushed it off as a kind gesture and just thanked him the next Sunday without ever getting the flower from my mother. It finally dawned on me that I might have missed a sign. So I called my mother and asked her what kind of flower it was. Without knowing that I had prayed a novena to Saint Thérèse, she casually responded, "Oh, it was one red rose."

Overcoming my reluctance to involve the saints in my prayer life led to the very thing I needed to heal my reluctance about leading Progressionista. Since then I have discovered that my leadership style as a woman aligns a lot with Saint Thérèse's "Little Way." Moments of big speeches and media interviews occur, but much of my work involves little roses: lifting boxes of books, cooking a meal for a board meeting at my home, and promising parents that their daughters will be just fine. I'm learning that there's always someone willing to give leaders too much praise or too much criticism. But I can always find purpose by leaning on God's understanding.

If you're someone in need of a sign from God, be sure you don't overlook the roses right in front of your eyes. Something in this world is waiting to be led by you. God has created a garden just for you to tend. And it's typically wrapped up in the small moments and obvious gifts that we fail to notice. After learning these lessons, I can now see the roses in Progressionista. They're in every girl who walks into a book club meeting, in every book I'm able to purchase, and in every woman who comes to speak to one of our groups. I just needed to let God open my eyes.

With love,
Shanel

If you're someone in need of a sign from God, be sure you don't overlook the roses right in front of your eyes.

♡ Shanel

SHANEL ADAMS is the founder of Progressionista, a library-based book club program in which girls meet a woman professional at each meeting and learn to love reading for leisure. Shanel started Progressionista in 2014 after attending Howard University and realizing how much leisure reading as a child had impacted her life. The program has introduced dozens of girls in Detroit, Michigan and Chicago, Illinois to many books and over seventy-five diverse women professionals. Progressionista also has given away over one thousand books to girls. Shanel's work inspired her to earn a master's in library services. She currently works as an elementary school teacher in Detroit.

Reflection Question and Prayer

"Saint Thérèse of Lisieux was the saint who eventually pushed me out of my quiet suspicion. She came out of nowhere."

Reflect on which saints have been close to you throughout your life. What have they taught you? Which of their qualities do you hope to live out in your own life?

Say a Hail Mary that you may grow in holiness and walk the path of sainthood. Then, close with this section's petition:

Saint Catherine of Siena, you devoted yourself to the sick, the suffering, and the spiritually needy. You also mediated disputes, brokered peace between warring factions, and provided guidance to popes and political leaders. Pray that if I am called to lead that I might do so in humility and with a spirit of Christ-like service to those in need. Amen.

Goodness Is Found
in the Moment

Dear Sister,

My husband and I celebrated our five-year wedding anniversary recently. That afternoon, while Steve was at work, I watched our wedding video for the umpteenth time. I cried. Not because it was beautiful in all the ways you might expect but because of one, very specific, heartbreaking detail: the interviews. Everyone's family wishes them well on their Most Special Day, but over and over again, captured for posterity I heard: "We can't wait for all the copper-colored, curly-haired babies!" We were vocal about our desire for children, and our joyful expectation was in full ripple effect at our wedding. But five years and three months since that day, the two babies we've conceived have gone to heaven before we could meet them. I'd be lying if I said it has been easy to exist in the waiting, especially as a Catholic woman.

Maybe your story isn't the same as mine, but I think we all have experienced the sting of loneliness, the uncertainty of those seasons, and the otherness of certain circumstances. It shapes us. Just as an artist touches a pencil to paper and creates a clear picture from sharp lines and deep shadows, the Lord is shaping us in his image. And it's in the making, in our surrender that we discover our identity in its truest form: as daughters of a loving Creator.

I remember the fall and winter of our first year of marriage like it was yesterday. Steve was working doubles between two jobs, and I was working full time in ministry. We were working opposite schedules to pay for treatment to help regulate my cycle and to increase our chances of conceiving. I worked mostly from home in a hideous pink fleece bathrobe that I'm sure killed the mood *plenty* of times. I binge-watched Netflix during my free time and had a monthly wine subscription that delivered bottles of reds and whites to our door; I was the only drinker in the house. My health was thrown to the wayside, I wasn't using a creative bone in my body, and my confidence plummeted. Then I hit yet another low point.

The morning of my grandmother's funeral, we had an appointment to see if the treatment I'd been taking had worked. We went dressed in black, which felt appropriate when the doctor told us it was a bust. I was not pregnant. I tried not to cry through my makeup as I dressed; I had a eulogy to give in an hour. Later that morning, I stood before the people who loved my Nana so dearly and did my best to honor her memory. My mind was elsewhere though, and my emotions all over the place. I was incredibly sad for so many reasons. The death of my grandmother, the disappointing news we had just received, and the overwhelming feeling of isolation closed in on me. It feels dramatic now, but I remember wondering what my legacy would be as a woman without children. I was throwing a pity party for one, and it was exhausting.

Then, I did what I always do when I'm trying to process my emotions—I wrote. As I scribbled my feelings onto paper, I wondered why I hadn't heard many women speaking out about infertility. It's a very private, personal issue, yet I wondered why it felt too taboo to even bring up. Were there other women out there like me, struggling in silence? Were they also wondering if they were the only ones? Soon I took my scribbles and typed them into cleaner lines on the computer, and then I made the decision to share our story on my blog. Somewhere in between my decision to share and publishing the actual words, however, fear found its way in.

For months I doubted myself and my motivations; I wondered if my words were better left unsaid. Would people think I was oversharing? What if I miraculously became pregnant in a few months and looked like a fraud? Would people think I hadn't struggled long enough to warrant such open, vulnerable disclosure? A year is nothing compared to ten. What if my sharing returned merely an echo of my own voice, further confirming that I was alone in my suffering? I offered my fears to God in prayer, asking for the right words at the right time, and I kept going. Finally, one September day, as I stood in the bedroom of our first apartment and hovered over the same keyboard I'm clacking on now, I read and reread endless edits of my first post. I knelt down, balancing my laptop on the corner of my bed in a familiar posture of prayer and breathed deeply: *Come, Holy Spirit. Lord, give me strength.* Then, I sent my story out into the world.

That day I never envisioned the immense response I would receive. I am amazed that so many women have felt comfortable sharing their stories with me after reading mine. But I am so honored they have. What a gift to be seen by women who've walked similar paths and bear similar battle scars. What a joy to lift one another other up even at a distance. Each time a woman shares her story with me or tells me that my words made her feel less alone, I say a prayer of thanksgiving. Because I have been in that place and other women were that point of connection for me that led me into deeper relationship with the Lord. And what greater responsibility do we have than to lead others to holiness? My online community also has helped me to learn more about the saints, beg prayers from strangers, and spend more time in front of the Blessed Sacrament, and it has given me a new song. That song is peace.

Social media has plenty of negative aspects but so much good can come of it too. Hearing the stories of women persevering through their trials is both powerful and humbling, and even more incredible is the ability we have to connect more deeply through a single message online. The Internet, in all its curated, two-dimensional, aesthetic glory, is still a community of people in need of care and connection. I think about this every time someone courageously comments on one of my posts or sends me a direct message. Before I respond, I ask myself, *How would I speak to my sister, my friend, to myself in this case? How does the Lord speak to me? What would Mary, in her infinite, motherly wisdom want me to say here?* Then, whether the conversation happens online or in real life, I know I'm being called further into my own unique femininity. The Lord always says, "Be. Listen. Love."

In the years since I first wrote that first post about infertility, it's strange to think back to that moment that changed everything. Before sharing my struggles, I felt so alone and purposeless. Every post I saw on social media—every baby announcement, new house, and fabulous vacation—made me feel inadequate. Comparing my real life to other peoples' digital dream lives was exhausting. All around me, women were stepping into their identity as mothers, and I felt left behind, even in my own community. I wondered where space for me could be found, *if* space for me even existed, especially in a Church so focused on the importance of family. I wondered who my people were and where I'd find purpose if I were to never become a parent. What would it mean for my own identity as a wife and a woman of faith?

In prayer, I asked God to show me his will for my life. I begged him to reveal my purpose in this season of life. I begged him not to allow me to be swallowed up in despair. I even tried irrational bargaining, "If you could just show me the future, this would be much easier. I could handle this if I knew what I was in for." As if prayer works like that. As if knowing each detail of my journey through years of infertility, including multiple miscarriages and more emotions than words can describe, would have helped me to be stronger emotionally, or more resolute in my calling, more whole. But you know as well as I do, that isn't the case. Knowledge of the future does not shield anyone from the living, breathing struggle of being human. Part of the beauty of living is the unknowing. It helps us to trust, to grow more fully into being our authentic selves, and it connects us to each other.

So often I've wished that this wasn't my cross to carry; I still have days when I feel this way. If I am being completely transparent, I never envisioned writing something like this. I thought my story would be one of brief trial and sure triumph. I thought we would have a baby in our arms at this point, and we could just forget any of this ever happened. The reality is that I'm still learning, still growing, still allowing myself to be vulnerable in real life and on the Internet. But I have found so much peace in surrendering the notion that goodness will come from *the next thing*. Goodness is found right here, in every moment, even in trials. I realize now, no matter what happens in the future, that this will always be a part of my story; it's paving the way for what's to come.

Sister, in these clouds of uncertainty, I've learned two alarmingly clear and important things: 1) I'm not defined by anything other than my identity in Christ, and 2) My story matters. Let go of the idea that a woman of faith has to fit a certain mold; let yourself live in true freedom. Let go of the lie that there isn't space for someone like you in the Church, simply because you don't fit the traditional definition of femininity. The Lord creates each unique individual woman for a purpose, and it's only through our feminine genius that our purpose is fulfilled. So, no more striving, no more hiding behind others' expectations. Instead, embrace the beauty of your individuality. You were created so meticulously, so intentionally by the Lord. The world doesn't need more ideas about what it means to be feminine, it needs our courage, our authenticity, and our boldness. It needs us to be truly who we are—daughters of the King.

Joyfully,

Katie

Let go of the idea that a woman of faith has to fit a certain mold; let yourself live in true freedom. Let go of the lie that there isn't space for someone like you in the Church, simply because you don't fit the traditional definition of femininity. The Lord creates each unique individual woman for a purpose, and it's only through our feminine genius that our purpose is fulfilled.

Katie

KATIE WALDOW is a wife, youth minister, and content creator who lives in Ocean City, New Jersey. Soon after writing this letter, Katie and her husband, Steve, found they were expecting. When she's not working, Katie can be found sipping iced lavender lattes, corralling her dog and two cats, and sharing her most embarrassing moments via Instagram. Her favorite ways to pray include the Divine Mercy Chaplet, Night Prayer, and learning praise and worship music on her pink ukulele. She loves sharing big ideas and going on surprise adventures. She dreams of one day converting an old house into a coffee shop. You can find out more about her at heykatie.co.

Reflection Question and Prayer

"The reality is that I'm still learning, still growing, still allowing myself to be vulnerable in real life and on the Internet. But I have found so much peace in surrendering the notion that goodness will come from *the next thing*. Goodness is found right here, in every moment, even in trials. I realize now, no matter what happens in the future, that this will always be a part of my story; it's paving the way for what's to come."

Do you spend a lot of time focused on *the next thing*? To practice surrendering to the present moment, write a list of things for which you're grateful. If you wrote down names of people you know, send them a note to let them know how grateful you are for their presence in your life.

Pray a Hail Mary for your growth in gratitude and for women and couples who struggle with infertility. Then, close with this section's petition:

Saint Catherine of Siena, you devoted yourself to the sick, the suffering, and the spiritually needy. You also mediated disputes, brokered peace between warring factions, and provided guidance to popes and political leaders. Pray that if I am called to lead that I might do so in humility and with a spirit of Christ-like service to those in need. Amen.

Leadership, Loneliness, and Friendship

Dear Sisters,

Once, while leading a small, women's prayer group, I decided to be honest and share a difficulty I was having in my marriage. Admitting that everything wasn't perfect and that I was really struggling was optional. I could have decided to just continue to present a buttoned-up version of myself. But we were sharing prayer requests, and my husband and I needed prayer. So I took a risk and unburdened my heart. After I shared, however, I felt a palpable shift in the room. I would love to say that I felt a rush of empathy or relief that someone was being vulnerable and honest. But I just saw eyes widen as an awkward silence descended on the room.

I had spent the year leading the same women in a Bible study, and we always closed our meetings with prayer requests. As we prayed for one another's intentions, I had challenged the women to ask for prayer for their own needs. This requires vulnerability, but when real needs were shared, we saw miracles as a result of our prayers. And our hearts were knit together in the process. Early prayer requests like "pray for my special intention" or "pray for my kids to have a good school year" had moved to honest admissions of unfulfilled longings, inner aches, and desperate needs.

So, why was the response to my prayer request so unlike the way the other women in the group had responded to one another? I was the leader. The other women were new to exploring their faith so perhaps it unsettled them to realize that God hadn't rewarded a faithful leader like me with a smooth road. At this point in their spiritual growth, these women needed me to model the difference Christ had made in my life. After all, if I was still having these sorts of difficulties even though I'd been committed to Christ for so many years, did he really make much of a difference?

I had started this small prayer group in part because I desired spiritual community. But things began to change as one small group grew into two, then four, then five.

> "We have all known the long loneliness and we have learned that the only solution is love and that love comes with community."[35]
>
> —Dorothy Day

What had begun as a small group I had hoped would meet my spiritual needs had turned into a national organization. Walking with Purpose now helps tens of thousands of women connect with Christ through Scripture. As Walking with Purpose grew, it helped many women, but I also lost the support I had longed to find. Each time I stepped into a higher leadership role, it became harder for my own spiritual needs to be met.

Leadership can be incredibly lonely, especially for women. I've spoken at conferences where I was the only female keynote speaker out of many. One could say that's an honor, but it's also isolating. What's more, when I leave my family at home to travel for work, I believe I face different challenges from men in similar situations. Maybe I sound overly traditional. I don't know. All I know is that when I leave for a work-related trip, I leave half my heart at home.

Female leaders in particular need a safe place where we can let down our guard, be honest, and share personal struggles and leadership challenges. But it's difficult to find a space to be authentic. We often say we value authenticity, but then we model a *curated* version of it. In social media photos, our jeans are ripped, our hair in a messy bun, and stuff is strewn on the counter. But we've also made sure the angle is just right to make us look both relatable and attractive. It's a fake authenticity, and it doesn't really satisfy.

We all need a small pack of friends who truly know our authentic selves, have our back, and speak grace-laced hard truths into our lives. Friends can be difficult to come by, but it's worth fighting for this kind of community. For a leader especially, these people can make the difference between burnouts and sustainable ministry. Taking off my leadership hat and just sitting down as messy-me with people I'm not leading has been critical to my emotional health. It's not that I'm not real with the people I lead. But often, the issues I struggle with involve the people I lead, so I need a neutral space where I can share candidly.

The ease of the friendships we made in elementary school ("You like that toy? Me too! Let's be friends!") becomes increasingly complicated as we get older. Suddenly, making friends takes serious effort because it requires spending time together. Accumulated shared hours naturally leads to a more thorough knowing of another person's life. And when we're in a school setting, all we have to do to accumulate hours with friends is to show up consistently. But once we are out of school, we have to put ourselves out there and proactively schedule the building of friendships. This is especially true when we move to a new area and have to start from scratch. In these situations, waiting around for someone to invite us somewhere is a recipe for isolation.

One time, after I had decided that I needed to be more intentional in forming friendships, I invited a woman to meet me for coffee. I knew she was an emotionally mature person who shared my love for the Lord. (Both are great things to look for if you are searching for a trustworthy friend.) So, I took a risk and opened up about my loneliness and my need to find a safe place to authentically share my heart. I asked her if she'd be willing to meet me each week to spend time talking about things that mattered to both of us. We explored questions like, *What are you dreaming about right now? What have been some of the most significant relationships in your life so far? If you could change one thing in the world, what would it be? What woman has most influenced your spiritual life, and why? What is God teaching you in this season of life?* Bit by bit, we shed our masks and built a fulfilling friendship.

Too often, we approach friendship with the idea that we'll just meet the perfect friend—people with whom we just click. We think that until those people show up, there's no point wasting time with others. I disagree. Good friends can come in packaging that disguises their potential. Sometimes a certain woman might not seem like an ideal friend at first. Give her a chance. Only by investing time do we see what kind of connection is possible. If you lead a group, your friendships will often have to be found outside, which isn't a failure on your part. It just means that you need a place where you can take off your "leadership hat" and just be you. You, in all your mess. You, with all your needs. You, with your both terrifying and exhilarating dreams. You, with your weariness from the burdens you carry as a leader.

You deserve to be known and seen—but not everyone has a right to hear your story. Choose the people you trust carefully. You don't need friends who just tell you what you want to hear. You need wise women who love you enough to tell you the truth, gently and directly. I'm thankful that, ever since high school, I have formed relationships with women who are more spiritually mature and often older than me. I invite these women to hold me accountable, and as I unload my heart, we sort things out together. When you find women who can hold sacred space for you, allowing you to honestly share what you are going through without judging or jumping in with a solution, you have struck gold. Friendship like that is a rare treasure.

I love the friendship of David and Jonathan in the Old Testament. They were able to call out the goodness in one another and stand by each other when circumstances threatened to destroy them. Even when God chose David to be the future king of Israel, that meant Jonathan would not ascend the throne, their friendship survived. David and Jonathan learned the secret of not competing or comparing and instead they championed one another. Scripture tells us, "The soul of Jonathan was bound to the soul of David, and Jonathan loved him as his own soul" (1 Sam 18:1, NRSV). My prayer for us is that we discover soul sisters—and that we link arms with one another, and don't let go.

In Christ,

Lisa

LISA BRENNINKMEYER is the founder and chief purpose officer of Walking with Purpose, a Catholic women's Bible study program. Raised an evangelical Protestant, she entered the Catholic Church in 1991. Her first book, *Walking with Purpose: Seven Priorities that Make Life Work*, has sold over seventy-five thousand copies. She is also the author of nine Bible studies for adult women, six studies for young women, and a program for middle school girls called Blaze. Lisa speaks internationally on a variety of topics, mainly pertaining to women and their spiritual journey. She and her husband, Leo, have seven children and live in Saint Augustine, Florida.

Dear Friend,

We often say we value authenticity, but then we model a **curated** version of it. In social media photos, our jeans are ripped, our hair is in a messy bun, and stuff is strewn on the counter. But we've also made sure the angle is just right to make us look both relatable and attractive. It's a fake authenticity, and it doesn't really satisfy. We all need a small pack of friends who truly know our authentic selves, have our back, and speak grace-laced hard truths into our lives.

Lisa Brenninkmeyer

Reflection Question and Prayer

"Too often, we approach friendship with the idea that we'll just meet the perfect friend—people with whom we just click. We think that until those people show up, there's no point wasting time with others. I disagree. Good friends can come in packaging that disguises their potential. Sometimes a certain woman might not seem like an ideal friend at first. Give her a chance. Only by investing time do we see what kind of connection is possible."

What are some ways you could take initiative to form community around you? Consider inviting some women you don't know very well for a meal so you can get to know them.

Pray a Hail Mary for prudence and wisdom regarding the women with whom God might be calling you to cultivate a friendship. Then, close with this section's petition:

Saint Catherine of Siena, you devoted yourself to the sick, the suffering, and the spiritually needy. You also mediated disputes, brokered peace between warring factions, and provided guidance to popes and political leaders. Pray that if I am called to lead that I might do so in humility and with a spirit of Christ-like service to those in need. Amen.

"I hid my talents for so long thinking that I was just trying to be humble, but it was actually because of fear."

Sarah Kroger

Becoming Brave

My dear sisters,

I've lived in fear for a lot of my life. I'm not proud of this, but it's a fact. Allow me to explain.

When I was younger, I was made fun of a lot. Armed with a wild imagination and a flair for the quirky, I tended to stand out from the rest of the kids in my class. On a day I'll never forget, one of the popular girls made fun of my shoes and called me a "giant loser" in front of the entire fourth-grade class. As I write now it sounds like such a trivial thing. And yet, even all these years later, I can still remember that feeling as if my ten-year-old heart were being completely destroyed. It's crazy how something terrible someone says to you as a kid can stick around. From that point on, I did everything in my power not to stand out. I tried my hardest to stay hidden and small to avoid ridicule and judgment.

From the time I was young, I knew I had a gift for music. My mom loves to share how I could match pitch before I could speak. I loved singing. But that bullying incident made me terrified of singing in front of people. Deep down I knew my voice was a precious gift from God, but the thought of people making fun of me was too much to bear. But as much as I tried, my love for music refused to be ignored.

In high school, I went on a youth retreat and found myself completely captivated by the worship. I had never felt God's love as close as I did when I prayed through the music. One of the team leaders gave a talk that was intended for the entire room, but in the moment it felt like he was talking directly to me. He said, "If you know you have a gift from God and you're not using it, you're denying the glory of God within you." Like a knife to the heart, I was pierced through and through. I knew that God was calling out to me. I had allowed fear and lies to get in the way of sharing a gift that was entrusted to me by him, and it was time to let it go.

Everything changed after that retreat. I was still terrified and would have done just about anything to avoid singing in front of a church full of people. But I was also convicted that I needed to do it. So, I did the unthinkable—I volunteered to cantor at Mass. Was I shaking all over? Absolutely. Did I sound like a dying donkey the first several weeks I sang because of my uncontrollable shaking? Yup. But I felt convicted, and a girl convicted by God is unstoppable. By God's grace, I kept showing up week after week, Sunday after Sunday. Little by little my courage started to build. Soon I started leading worship at my youth group. Then, the youth group down the road invited me to lead worship. Then a church across state asked me to come, and things continued to grow from there. God kept opening doors and invited me to walk through them, and my courage grew with each "yes."

I now lead worship in churches around the world as a full-time ministry. You would think after all these years of experience that I would be totally confident every time I walk on stage or release an album. Unfortunately, that's not true. Sometimes I still get unbearably nervous. At times, I would rather hide behind a bush than sing in front of people. I continue to sing my way through fear. Why? Because I'm a broken human being learning how to be brave.

As a woman working in a male-dominated industry, I often end up in situations where I need to be brave. I automatically stand out, and I'm learning how to embrace that reality rather than run from it. To be an artist means that you create something meant to be shared with the world. That takes bravery and vulnerability. Bravery and vulnerability don't seem like they would naturally go together, but they do. To be vulnerable literally means "to be woundable." You have to be brave in order to be vulnerable with other people; and you have to be vulnerable to share your art with the world.

A very important lesson I've had to learn is that the art I create and how it's received doesn't define me. It's a massive part of who I am, but it doesn't define me. I'll never forget the first time I received a bad review of one of my songs. The reviewer wasn't cruel in the commentary, but the person just hadn't connected with and interpreted the song in the way I had intended. If I allow my art to define me, negative reviews would ruin me. The thing is, not everyone will understand or relate to what I create. But that doesn't mean they don't understand or relate to me as a human. I'm not defined by what other people say or think about me. I'm defined by what God says about me. When our identity is rooted in our identity as beloved daughters of God, bravery and vulnerability follow.

Another important lesson I've learned is that humility is not the same as hiding. For many years, I hid my talents from others. Mainly because I hated the idea of self-promotion. It can feel so contrary to everything we know humility to be. One summer in college I served as a missionary at a youth camp. Every week, a new worship leader would join us to lead worship. And every week I would actively avoid the musician as the rest of the staff would hound the person to have me sing with him or her. It drove me crazy. But the wild thing is that one of those worship leaders stayed in touch with me. And a year later that person produced my first album and became my mentor in songwriting and leading worship. God works in mysterious ways indeed.

I hid my talents for so long thinking that I was just trying to be humble, but it was actually because of fear. I feared that I was too much or not enough; that people wouldn't like what they heard; that I wasn't holy enough to lead worship; that my pride would take over if I didn't actively work to stay hidden, etc. The fears were endless. But, when lies start swirling, the truth I desperately try to hold onto is this—fear is not of God. God is love, and 1 John 4:18 tells us, "There is no fear in love, but perfect love drives out fear." We weren't made to live in fear.

If I had the power to show my sixteen-year-old self a glimpse of what my life looks like now, I know she wouldn't believe me. The places I've traveled. The people I've met. The community to

"Does not Wisdom call,
and Understanding raise her voice?
On the top of the heights along the road,
at the crossroads she takes her stand;
By the gates at the approaches of the city,
in the entryways she cries aloud:
'To you, O people, I call;
my appeal is to you mortals.
You naive ones, gain prudence,
you fools, gain sense.
Listen! for noble things I speak;
my lips proclaim honest words.
Indeed, my mouth utters truth,
and my lips abhor wickedness.
All the words of my mouth are sincere,
none of them wily or crooked;
All of them are straightforward to
the intelligent,
and right to those who
attain knowledge.
Take my instruction instead of silver,
and knowledge rather than
choice gold.'"

—Proverbs 8:1–10

which I belong. The songs I've written and co-written. The worship I've helped to lead. All the blessings that make up my life today would be gone in an instant if I had allowed my fears to stand in the way. And sister, let me tell you, I was so close to letting it all slip away! I *still* struggle with fear. And what terrifies me most is I sometimes still allow my fears to become an obstacle. I wonder how my fears continue to keep me from becoming the person I am meant to become.

When I feel consumed by fear, I try to look to Mary as a source of inspiration. Think about it, she was the world's first true worship leader! Her entire life was a song that pointed to her Son. She leads us all directly to Jesus' Sacred Heart. Whether or not you're a worship leader, all women have a unique calling and ability to lead people to the Heart of Christ. If you take away nothing else from this letter, I hope you will allow these words to sink into your soul. You are loved. You belong to God. He has given you gifts that only you can share with the world in your own unique way. When you don't share your gifts, the whole world misses out on your unique communication of God's glory. You are not defined by your past mistakes or the lies you may have been told. You are who God says you are. I hope you never forget that.

Shine bright, my sisters, because that's what you were made to do.

Sarah

Sarah Kroger is a worship leader and songwriter originally from Melbourne, Florida. She has led worship and shared her music at many national and international events for over a decade. Her tender heart of prayer combined with her rare vocal talent makes for a unique and intimate experience of prayer everywhere she goes. Sarah's passion is to create a safe and prayerful space through her music in which people can encounter the heart of God in a profound way. Her latest full-length album, "Bloom," recently was released through Integrity Music. When Sarah isn't on the road, she lives in Nashville, Tennessee with her husband, Dom.

Reflection Question and Prayer

"The fears were endless. But, when lies start swirling, the truth I desperately try to hold onto is this—fear is not of God. God is love, and 1 John 4:18 tells us, 'There is no fear in love, but perfect love drives out fear.' We weren't made to live in fear."

To step into your unique calling can take serious courage. Where do you struggle with courage the most in your life? Brainstorm simple ways you can practice the virtue of courage in your daily life.

Pray a Hail Mary for growth in courage for yourself and for women everywhere. Pray that all women may step courageously into God's unique calling for their lives. Then, close with this section's petition:

Saint Catherine of Siena, you devoted yourself to the sick, the suffering, and the spiritually needy. You mediated wars, brought peace, and provided guidance to popes and political leaders. Pray that when I'm called to lead, I may lead with humility and a spirit of Christ-like servitude to those in need.

Finding Your Path
in the Church

Hey there,

When I converted to Catholicism in 1998, I was full of a boisterous and somewhat obnoxious delight in the Church. At the time I exuberantly told my best friend that as a Catholic, "My worldview is so unified!" One of the great blessings of friendship is that she has made fun of me for this for over twenty years.

Sometimes it can feel like the Catholic Church hands us an intricate object with interlocking pieces that—if handled correctly—will all fall into place, and our faith will form a perfect, beautiful sphere. We often buy into this misconception when we suggest that our faith gives us answers to all life's questions. Or when we think that being Catholic is great because we'll always have clear guidance in everything we do. God responds to all we ask, but that response is often far more covert and troubling than the "answers" we were seeking. Catholics sometimes act like we're offering people life's rulebook, rather than an entrance into mystery. Formed by these assumptions as a new convert, I often accepted simplistic guidance for myself and offered it to others.

Then my life offered me several experiences that didn't fit easy certainties and clear categories. I couldn't imagine what it would look like to bring all these wild, weird, harrowing experiences to the altar. I was very lucky that God gave me a certain willful stubbornness that didn't allow me much room for existential doubt. But because certain urgent aspects of my life and my calling from God hadn't been modeled by the Catholics around me, I began to feel like I was locked out of that small, perfect sphere of faith. I was sure that in Christ is found freedom and in the Church is found refuge—so why did the easy, confident answers begin to sound like traps?

I spent about a decade and a half bringing my out-of-control drinking to the confessional and wondering why nothing ever got better. Some priests tried their best to give me good advice. One suggested inpatient rehab. Another, more confident that he had answers, told me I *had to* go to Alcoholics Anonymous every day for a week. I wasn't sure if that was part of my penance, so I did it. One hour every day, while morbidly sucking on my hangover coffee, I listened to people tell stories to which I was supposed to relate. Instead I felt nothing except *All these people are better than me* (which turns out to be the kind of thought one has right before buying another bottle of bottom-shelf bourbon).

Today I've pieced together seven years of sobriety. And if the pieces don't seem to others to fit together the way they should, I don't care. I love the Twelve Steps; I still don't do meetings. I started going to daily Mass, which helped. (And then I stopped, and now I'm trying to start again.) My experience of addiction has been intensely spiritual (rather than, for example, psychological); but even when I talk with people who need what AA calls a "spiritual solution," it's often easier to see the differences in our experiences than the similarities. It doesn't matter. God didn't give me their recovery. He has as many different paths to hope as people in despair.

On a less intense note, I have many friends who love Eastern liturgies, spiritualities, and styles of worship— some Orthodox and some in Byzantine or Melkite churches in communion with Rome. I've loved learning about the diversity of Christian worship, the diversity of beauty available to us, and the diversity of languages we can use to articulate our faith. It turns out, however, that I'm desperately Western. I love gory Spanish crucifixes, Saint Anselm and Saint Bernard, statues and holy cards, Eucharistic adoration and Corpus Christi processions. One of my favorite memories of church music is hearing "Amazing Grace" played on a Casio keyboard—it should have been so chintzy, yet it was so haunting! I doubt there's a document from the Vatican explaining why that was so good.

The Faith is more complex and stranger than any precision-tooled theology can express. The kinds of Catholicism you were raised with aren't the only kinds, and the vocations of the people who brought you into the Church aren't the only paths of love. For instance, when I became Catholic, all the other Catholics I knew were straight. I didn't know any other gay people who were willing to accept the Church's sexual ethic. I didn't even know *of* anybody like that. For all my talk of how Catholicism had a unified worldview, there seemed to be no place for me—especially for my longing to love and serve other women in the Church. I acted like being Catholic gave me all the answers when in fact I wasn't even sure how to ask the questions.

As a gay woman, I've had to rediscover forgotten ways of love, like Scriptural practices of lifelong same-sex love. In contemporary culture, terms like "intimacy," "devotion," "commitment," and even "love" itself are often used as mere euphemisms for sexual relationships, leaving gay Christians unsure how our own desires could ever be lived in harmony with God's will. And yet both Scripture and Christian history offer examples of people whose love of another man or woman was intense, devoted, and chaste; self-giving, life-shaping; passionate, sacrificial, and beautiful. For example, the covenant between David and Jonathan (see 1 Sam 18:3) or the promises made by Ruth to Naomi (see Ruth 1:16-17). Saint Gregory of Nazianzus describes his friendship with Saint Basil the Great as being like "one soul inhabiting two bodies."[37] Their friendship, in which they rejoiced in one another's progress in the spiritual life, drew each of them closer to Christ as well as to one another. Saint Frances of Rome had a life-shaping partnership with her sister-in-law Vannozza. Together the two went to Mass, prayed in a secret chapel they set up, and served the poor and imprisoned.

When gay people come to the Church for guidance, too often we're urged to flee from any kind of same-sex love—especially anything we think of as committed, intimate, or devoted. Anything we do to deepen these loves is seen as solely an occasion of sin. This attitude of suspicion damages gay people's faith: how can you know yourself as a child of God when everyone around you treats you as a walking sexual time bomb? And it ignores the havens our faith can offer for same-sex love that is both chaste and committed, both celibate and intimate, a path to holiness for those who love God and one another.

Contemporary Christians—including many gay and lesbian believers—are reviving old Christian practices like covenants or blessings for friendship. We are finding ways to let our love of someone of the same sex be a pathway to Christ and not a barrier to following him. Led by these models from the Christian past, we are leading the Church as a whole to rediscover the beauty of friendship and the many other Christian forms of kinship that go beyond the nuclear family.

One of the greatest ongoing joys of my life in the Church has been learning how many ways we can pour ourselves out in love. Marriage and religious vows aren't the only Catholic forms of love, service, kinship, or community. If you need a different form of love—a different shape for your life and your future—you can be certain that God will help you. There will be a path for you, even if it's hidden, even if it takes a long time to find, and even if your Catholic friends or family find it difficult to understand. An unusual path requires unusual courage and trust, but it will also bring unusual joys and unexpected companions on the way.

The places where I'm still working out what God wants for me—including in my deepest friendships—are places where I "walk by faith" (see 2 Cor 5:7). They're places where I know I have to trust God, so I cling closer to him in recognition of my dependence. I've had to learn that faith doesn't always make my life or choices simple and obvious. It leads me to trust that God is there even when I don't understand how to serve him.

Sometimes I still wish I could present my faith to others as a perfect shining sphere. I am embarrassed by the thought that my life might not be enviable. I might want to be a good example for others, but I keep turning into a cautionary tale. I still regularly face uncertainty, weakness, and failure (though it's often in these moments that I learn some humility and compassion for others). But again and again I've learned that other people need my rough edges, weirdness, unanswered questions, and unslaked longings. The perfect shining sphere can be inspiring—but it's also intimidating. It's hard to imagine being like those people whose faith seems to fit so easily into the grooves of their lives. (And, honestly, those people probably feel the same way. Who really feels like they're living a picture-perfect, #soblessed life?) Our difficulties and uncertainties are often places from which we witness most clearly—because then our actions are rooted in trust in God and not in the knowledge of what he has planned.

Your life may seem like a chaotic mix of irreconcilable elements. Over time, however, if you submit yourself to the Church's teachings—and trust that she is weird enough to find a place for your weirdness—a path may start to emerge from the chaos. Or you might never recognize the path you're walking. You might never be sure what God wants for you. But you can be sure that he doesn't want just the parts of your life that fit together, the parts that make sense, the parts you can present confidently to the outside world. He wants *all* of you.

In love and trouble,

Eve Tushnet

EVE TUSHNET is a writer and speaker living in her hometown of Washington, D.C. She entered the Catholic Church in 1998, at the ripe old age of nineteen. She is the author of *Gay and Catholic: Accepting My Sexuality, Finding Community, Living My Faith* as well as two novels, *Amends,* and *Punishment: A Love Story*. Eve is also the editor of *Christ's Body, Christ's Wounds: Staying Catholic When You've Been Hurt in the Church*. She writes about everything from little-known punk movies to medieval penitential practices.

Your life may seem like a chaotic mix of irreconcilable elements. Over time, if you submit yourself to
the Church's teachings — & trust that She is weird enough
to find a place for your weirdness — a path may start
to emerge from the chaos. Or you might never recognize
the path you're walking. You might never be completely
sure what God wants for you. But you can be sure that
He doesn't want just the parts of your life that fit
together, the parts that make sense, the parts you can
present confidently to the outside world. He wants all
of you.

Reflection Question and Prayer

"I've had to learn that faith doesn't always make my life or choices simple and obvious. It leads me to trust that God is there even when I don't understand how to serve him."

In what aspects of your life do you find it hard to see God's grace? Perhaps it's in a strange or strained relationship, a difficult experience, or an odd thought or doubt you can't shake. Take a moment to talk to God about it in prayer—as honestly as you can—and ask for the grace to see a path forward.

Then, say a Hail Mary for all who feel out of place at times in Catholicism, that they may find a home and a path within the Church. Then, close with this section's petition:

Saint Catherine of Siena, you devoted yourself to the sick, the suffering, and the spiritually needy. You also mediated disputes, brokered peace between warring factions, and provided guidance to popes and political leaders. Pray that if I am called to lead that I might do so in humility and with a spirit of Christ-like service to those in need. Amen.

"There is neither Jew nor Greek, there is neither slave nor free person, there is not male and female; for you are all one in Christ Jesus."

—Galatians 3:28

Receive

Taking a phone call at an inconvenient time from a struggling friend

Meeting Jesus face to face in adoration

Starting a conversation with a stranger in a room full of unfamiliar faces

In this section, we'll examine how femininity can be expressed through genuine receptivity to persons. In these letters, Catholic women from a wide variety of backgrounds reflect on how they have become more open-armed and loving through their particular circumstances and sufferings.

Julie Lai

Julie shares how her experience as a Vietnamese-American Catholic woman in a predominantly white Catholic community has helped her to see the importance of the universality of the Church.

Kate Capato

Kate shares how she has been inspired to receive and give Christ by Mary's healing and comforting presence in her life.

Emily Fossier

Emily shares her journey as a mother with mental illness and how accepting this cross has helped her to glorify God and love her family.

Alexa Hyman

Alexa shares what it was like to become pregnant as a single woman and how motherhood has challenged her to be more open to God's love.

Meg-Hunter Kilmer

Meg-Hunter shares how the broken plans that she continually encounters as a wandering missionary who lives out of her car have taught her to be a better listener.

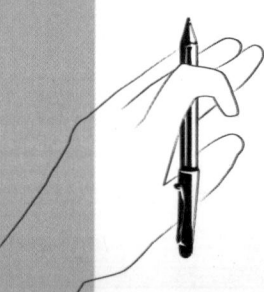

Mary, Mother of the Church

The patron saint for this section is Mary, Mother of the Church. She is the model par excellence of receptivity and open-armed, authentic love of the other, especially those in need. Such a love can only grow if it's rooted in a sincere, ever-deepening openness to Jesus Christ. Indeed, Mary was the first person to whom Jesus' mission and identity were revealed, the first to receive him, and truly, the first witness of God's abundant love. When the angel Gabriel appeared to her, announcing that she would become the Mother of God, Mary humbly and freely gave her consent—her *fiat*—to receive Christ as her son. This private, startling conversation between an angel and a young Jewish teenage woman led to the Incarnation of the Son of God who would save humankind.

In her choice to accept God's will and to become the Mother of God, we can recognize Mary as a truly free woman. She was free to recognize, choose, and receive the good that God offered to her in the moment of the Annunciation. Mary's freedom is perfected by her lack of *original sin*—the deprivation of original holiness that we inherit from Adam and Eve's sin. Original sin prevents us from true fellowship with God—from becoming fully alive women and men—as it wounds our human nature and cannot be erased without Baptism.

Because God completely preserved Mary from original sin, we can be tempted to see her as an alien or superhuman. Perhaps more for women than men, Mary can seem quite unrelatable and inaccessible in her perfection. She is not inhuman in her perfection, however, rather she is *more* human. Mary is humanity *restored*. God created us to be holy. Sin isn't a defining feature of human nature but rather a loss of who we are, something that can only be found again in Christ. Sin doesn't make us more human; it prevents us from becoming who we were truly created to be—women and men able to always recognize, choose, and receive the will of God. Just like Mary.

Mary is the human person fully alive. Her choice to receive God into her womb enabled each of us is able to come to know Jesus Christ, the incarnate Son of God. Her *fiat* turned the key to open the gates of heaven for us. Thus, Mary models how we are called to receive Christ in all aspects of our lives so that in and through him we might receive both ourselves and others. In the coming letters, you'll find examples of authentic, bold Marian receptivity as well as corresponding quotes, questions, and writing-space for you to prayerfully reflect on how you can live this quality out in your own life.

PRAYER TO MARY

Mary, my Mother and friend, please ask God to grant me the grace to respond to his will with a generous "yes" and to receive his great love for me so that I may share it with others.

Amen.

Keep the Door Open

Hi friend,

It's nice to meet you through this letter. I wonder what it would be like if we were to meet in real life. *How would I see you? How would you see me? What kind of person would you hope I'd be?*

Recently, I went to a young adult, Catholic event. Eager to deepen my faith and build friendships, I sat down at a table and tried to get to know the people around me. I was in mid-conversation with another person when a religious sister leaned over to me and said, "My religious order has a convent in Korea." It took me a minute to process why she had told me this piece of information. But then I knew why. She only saw me as Asian. She didn't ask me my name, what school I went to, or wait to have a conversation long enough to learn that I am actually Vietnamese. I felt reduced to my race—dehumanized and foreign to her, I felt like I was at a ritzy party and someone had asked how I got invited. The underlying message I heard was that I don't belong.

The word "catholic" means "universal" and rightly so; the Church is universal. But sometimes it doesn't feel that way.

One of my favorite images of the Church is the columns at Saint Peter's Basilica in Vatican City. Shaped like open arms, they represent the Church's maternal embrace, welcoming everyone in. I can't think of anything more cross-cultural, unified, or larger than the Church. Like heartbeats in unison, approximately 350,000 Masses are celebrated every day around the world. The same readings, the same Mass parts, the same celebration of the Eucharist. It's incredible to think how deeply connected I am to billions of strangers across the world through this shared mystery.

But, from where my feet walk in the world, it's hard to remember sometimes that the Church is universal. The Church I experience daily in my local Catholic community isn't the Vatican. My community is Saint Christopher's parish down the street, a diocesan young adult retreat, a national conference, and different Catholic media platforms. In these places, the Church doesn't always feel universal. Often, I feel foreign, out of place. So much so that sometimes I'm surprised when I remember that the Church didn't start in Europe or North America.

Of course, no one walks up to me and says, "You don't belong in the Church because you're Asian." But it's a message I hear softly whispered in little ways: the choice to highlight and display certain European saints over and over rather than the many others from other continents; the people who are chosen as leaders and speakers at big events; subtle suggestions that some political stances are okay, and some are absolutely not; the painfully racist jokes I've heard Catholics tell; the kinds of questions I'm asked. So much of my life is devoted to the Church, yet it somehow can still feel like I'm stepping into someone else's space and assimilating to someone else's culture. And when this happens, it's easy to begin to feel like Jesus isn't my God—like he belongs to someone else. Or like he's just a cultural icon rather than a living and breathing God-man from Nazareth who desires my heart too.

After feeling for some time like my Asian identity and my faith were mutually exclusive, I found myself struggling. I love the Lord and my faith, but I was hurt. So, I went to an adoration chapel. I walked in, sat on the floor, and said to the Lord with a tired voice, "I'm having a hard time loving the Church." After a brief silence between us, I felt the Father respond, "Well, I don't have a hard time loving the Church, because Julie, you are the Church." I realized in that moment that when I looked at the Church, I was focusing on the scandals, corruption, and power dynamics. But God was reminding me that when he sees the Church, he sees me.

I was stunned. I couldn't believe God could see the Church, the Body of Christ, in the face of a twenty-three-year-old Vietnamese-American woman. I felt so seen. I had felt so apart from the Church. My face was never the face I had pictured when I thought of a Catholic person. But I realized in that moment that I wasn't a guest; I was home. I wasn't partaking in someone else's Church; I am the Church. That call from the Father helped me to I realize that I needed to do my part to cultivate a

"The person is a kind of good to which only love constitutes the proper and fully-mature relation."[39]

—Saint John Paul II

home in the Church for others. I do this by giving my whole self—my race, age, laity, womanhood, story, and receptive heart—to hold open a door for others to come in.

The Church's universality is so much more than an opportunity for multilingual diversity or a cultural festival with food and flags. Universality is our name. Universality is our call. Universality is the open arms of the Church; we are called to be all-embracing and to welcome in everyone and anyone. It's about inviting every person into the Church. The Church's universality begs me to come out of my bubble to see the whole Church across the globe, in all her varied faces and experiences.

Universality is about expanding my heart to fit the whole world within it. The Church's universality not only asks me to see the whole Church but to see each whole person in front of me. It's so easy to reduce people to the parts with which I feel most comfortable. But true Christ-like love receives people totally for who they are and as they are, without invalidation. Very simply, universality beholds the sacredness, the very image of God in the person in front of me. Universality is about meeting people with open arms so that they can come to know the Church as home. Universality is about showing people the love God has for them.

Friend, the truth is that the doors of the Church are heavy, and I'm becoming weary from holding them open. But I don't think it has to be this way. It wasn't meant to be this way. So I send you this letter, humbly asking you to stand next to me holding open the Church's doors.

With love,

Julie Bao Yen Lai

JULIE LAI is a young adult living in San Diego, California. She spent a few years working in ministry and Catholic media. Nowadays she is working toward her licensure as a marriage and family therapist. She wants to spend her whole life growing more in awe of the sacredness of the human person, and she hopes to walk with others toward hope, healing, and freedom. In her free time, you can find her enjoying a picnic, taking photos, writing in a coffee shop, or watching a sunset.

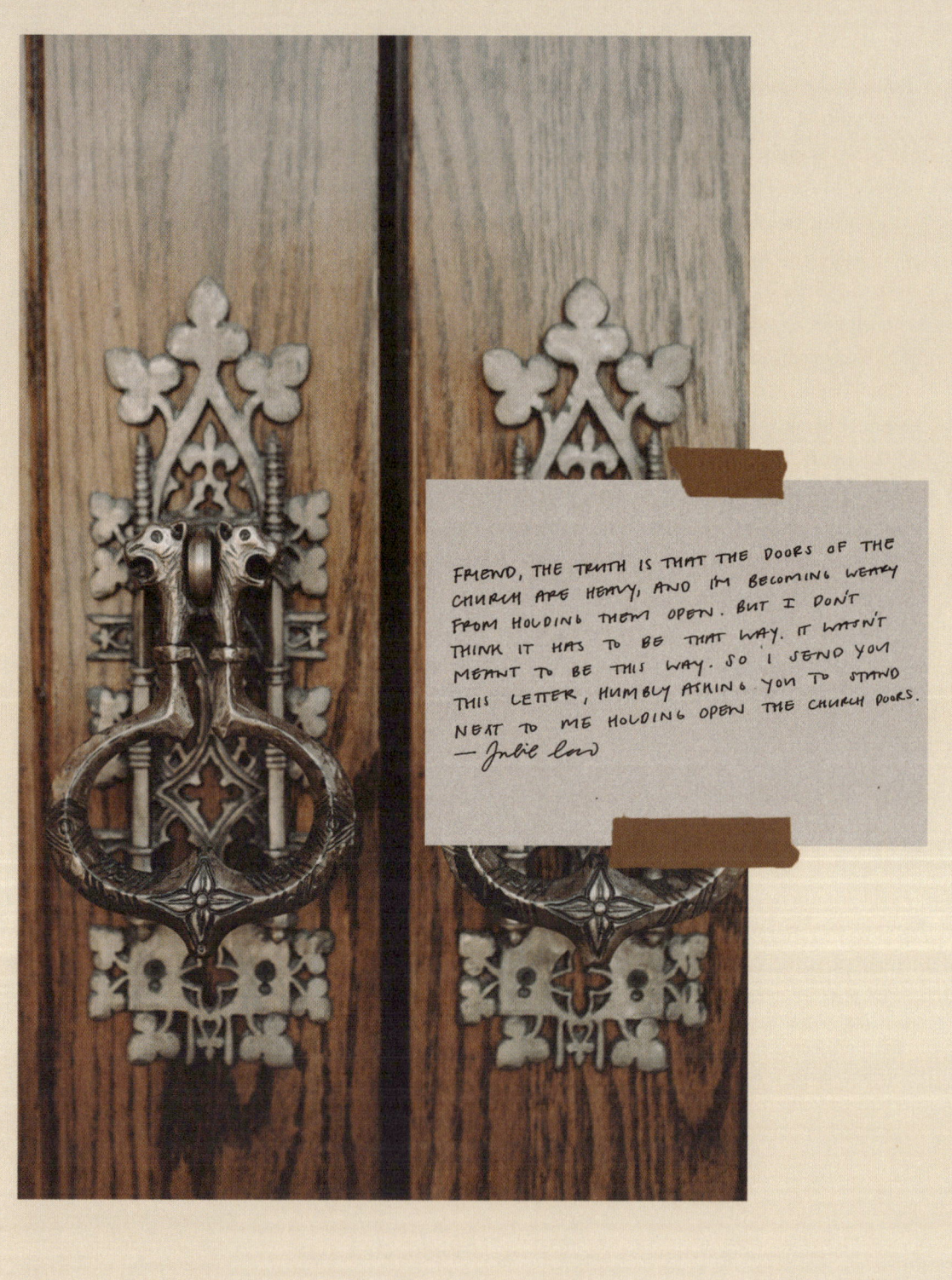

FRIEND, THE TRUTH IS THAT THE DOORS OF THE CHURCH ARE HEAVY, AND I'M BECOMING WEARY FROM HOLDING THEM OPEN. BUT I DON'T THINK IT HAS TO BE THAT WAY. IT WASN'T MEANT TO BE THIS WAY. SO I SEND YOU THIS LETTER, HUMBLY ASKING YOU TO STAND NEXT TO ME HOLDING OPEN THE CHURCH DOORS.
— Julie Law

Reflection Question and Prayer

"It's so easy to reduce people to the parts with which I feel most comfortable. But true Christ-like love receives people totally for who they are and as they are, without invalidation. Very simply, universality beholds the sacredness, the very image of God in the person in front of me."

Think about the people you encounter throughout your week: maybe the baristas at your favorite coffee shop, family members, the cashier at the grocery store. Consider some small ways that you could love them better.

Pray a Hail Mary asking that you may be an instrument of Christ's peace and unity within the world. Then, close with this section's petition:

Mary, my Mother and friend, please ask God to grant me the grace to respond to his will with a generous "yes" and to receive his great love for me so that I may share it with others. Amen.

"This Is My Daughter"

Hello Dear,

I write to you as a newly married woman! It's such a gift to enter into my vocation; marriage united with Christ is always good. When I'm not spending time with my sweet husband, my days are filled with painting sacred art in my new home studio. At times, I even get to travel and give presentations on the power of beauty while choreographing dances to compliment this message. Essentially, I live a very artistic life (thankfully, my husband is an artist too so he enjoys every bit of it).

Today I want to share with you something rather heavy that I experienced that has been made new. I have often wished that I could change many moments from my past, but I never could, and I still can't. Not too long ago, feelings of guilt, shame, and confusion surfaced in my heart from things that happened years ago. Others could not understand my personal suffering. After all, only I experienced it, and, honestly, it's still difficult for me to explain. It began many years ago when I was living in India doing missionary work. There I encountered a long spiritual darkness and a great confusion that I now know was a spiritual attack. As I sought to find my way in life, the darkness overwhelmed me. It seemed as if every step I took just led me down a darker path. Fear of God and distrust grew in my once carefree heart. It became harder and harder to say "yes" to God.

I went to India intending to teach dance and art to the beautiful children there. All I wanted to do was to use my artistic talents to help others. Yet, what I experienced instead haunted me for years and caused great pain for a long, long time. This time of darkness made me feel completely abandoned by God, and I made decisions during this time that I don't think I would have made otherwise. Unfortunately, when I talked to family and friends about what I was experiencing, they could not really understand, and this made the pain even stronger.

Fast forward a bit. A few years after I got back from India, I met a handsome musician named Peter, and we immediately connected. I am convinced that Our Lady chose the moment we were engaged. Because of his Polish heritage, Peter intended to propose to me in front of an image of Our Lady of Czestochowa at a local shrine. Due to a Mass in progress, he ended up proposing to me in front of an image of Our Lady of Guadalupe in a side chapel. Little did we know but there was great meaning and joy in that slight difference. Honestly, it was as if Our Lady of Guadalupe picked us. Do you know much about the miracle of Our Lady of Guadalupe? It's a powerful story, and one that I am always learning more about.

In 1531, the Blessed Mother appeared in Mexico several times to an indigenous man named Juan Diego. At one point, Mary asked Juan Diego to visit the local bishop to convince him to build a church in her honor. While he is standing before the skeptical bishop, Juan Diego opens his cloak and roses fall out (in the middle of December!). A miraculous image of the Blessed Mother also had appeared on Juan Diego's cloak as a sign. The cloak still exists to this day and can be seen in the Basilica of Our Lady of Guadalupe in Mexico City. Every symbol on the cloak is meaningful. I could go on all day about this, but I'll just explain a few. Researchers have discovered that the stars on the cloak are the exact constellation of the stars on the very day the image appeared. Not to mention, the pattern of the stars and flowers on the cloak form a musical score for a heavenly melody. Mary's hair in the image is parted in the center and is a sign of her virginity, and the ribbon around her waist is tied in a way that shows that she is with child. She stands in front of rays as a sign that she bears God within her and is therefore greater than the Aztec sun god the people worshipped at the time. Even more amazingly, it's said that the position of her legs show that she is dancing! As I mentioned, my husband Peter is a musician, and I paint and am a dancer as well so this symbolism was particularly meaningful to us.

Ever since our engagement, Our Lady of Guadalupe continues to pop up in all sorts of places that we do not expect. She doesn't just come to us in times of joy, she is also present in times of great pain. One Sunday afternoon, she came to me when I was sitting in Mass. I had been experiencing that same sadness I felt in India. For some reason, during Mass, it had resurfaced in my heart. (The evil one likes to distract and bring fear, doubt, guilt, and ugly lies to our minds, especially during Mass.) This particular Sunday I was at a Polish Mass with Peter and his family. I don't speak Polish so it was hard for me to follow everything that was going on. I spent the Mass crying out to Jesus and showing him the lies about my worth and value that were circling in my mind. I felt like I was no longer good enough to be a follower of Christ, that I had failed as a saint in the making. I was believing the lie that I was on my own in life and that every choice was just an opportunity for me to fail again.

Yet, this particular Sunday in a beautiful Polish church, something changed. The white-walled church was filled with depictions of Polish saints, and the pews contained many Polish families, but Our Lady of Guadalupe was also there! It was just a "guest visit" so to speak. Her image was traveling around and was in the church temporarily. But of course she would be there when we were. As the past weighed me down, I stared in pain at the image of Our Lady of Guadalupe in the church. She looked like she was arrayed in light. My heart didn't understand the pain that was suffocating my mind, and I was not sure what to do. Yet, when I looked at Mary, a sudden strength and peace powerfully overcame me. I felt my Mama speak to my bleeding heart. Gently she said, "I know what you felt. I know your pain. I understand your confusion then and now, and I, your Mother, am here." As tears fell down my cheek, I then felt Mary wrap me in her mantle of deep, deep love and hope. Even now, as I write this memory, I am weeping. Her gentle presence that day was unmistakable.

After that day I kept going over and over that stunning encounter in my mind. I was convinced that it was not only meant for me to experience. So I decided to paint it. Over the next few months, I prayed with the message I had received from Mary and discerned how best to portray it. As I prayed, Eve came to my mind. I couldn't imagine the weight that she and Adam must have felt years later after the fall that had changed the course of history. I mean, think about it, their sin cursed the rest of humankind forever. I would have been so heavy with guilt. Another source of inspiration for me was the image of the Pieta, Our Lady holding and embracing the dead body of Christ after the crucifixion. I could imagine Mama Mary in that position holding her other children—just as she had held me that day. As I painted, I pondered all of these things and soon the image I titled "The Woman" was created.

"While [Jesus] was speaking, a woman from the crowd called out and said to him, 'Blessed is the womb that carried you and the breasts at which you nursed.' He replied, 'Rather, blessed are those who hear the word of God and observe it.'"

—Luke 11:27–28

Many people are brought to tears when I show them my painting of Our Lady of Guadalupe gently holding and embracing the naked Eve. They are moved to see Mary covering up and embracing Eve's nude body as if to say, "This is my daughter." It's a moment of protection just as much as it is of mercy. When I watch people look at this painting, I can see how much others need to experience their Mama too. I can see it in their eyes. They have pain; we all do. Yet, just as in the painting Mary pulls Eve toward her womb where Christ resides, our heavenly Mother knows how to pull us closer to Christ to be healed.

Oh what a gift of grace! What an honor to share this image of Mary's motherhood with the little talent I have. I really hope that everyone who sees this painting will put themselves in the place of Eve. No matter their past, regret, or hurt. Don't you agree? Maybe you have regret too. Possibly due to something you chose knowingly or unknowingly. Maybe because of something that was done to you that you could not prevent. No matter what it may be, I pray that we can let go of our past and surrender it all to Jesus through Mary to be redeemed and healed. Just as Eve rests in her Mother's embrace in my painting and finally stops trying to be in control.

Hope and redemption are always possible. As a sign of this, in the bottom corner of my painting is a bitten apple and a white rose growing out of it. The bitten apple reminds us of the moment Adam and Eve distrusted the Lord and chose their own path. And the white rose is a sign of purity and is often used as a symbol of Mary, Mother of God. Mary, truly pure and untainted, fully lived out her constant "yes" to our Savior. No matter what. Beauty can come from what seems to be forever lost, through letting our grasp of it go and saying yes to Christ. Dear sister, nothing is lost or without hope when we give it over to Christ. Even huge sins can be made new if we confess and give them over to our heavenly Father and to Mary, our Mother.

As women, we are all called to bring others close to our hearts and to share what has been given to us by God. We are called to help grow and cultivate that seedling of hope that resides in our neighbor. Through painting this experience, I felt able to collaborate with God and to invite others more deeply into his heavenly love. That pain that I had felt for many years has lessened as I have allowed myself to be held by my Mother Mary, to surrender to her embrace. God took my past and is making it new. A lot of us struggle to let go of control as women; this was my problem and sometimes still is. I was trying to be my own savior. Mary gracefully came to me to show me that a posture of trust is what would open me to Jesus' saving grace. It's a posture that I must keep learning and painting my experience has helped me to continue to learn it.

All of my work as an artist is a way to share what God is doing in my life. My paintings, choreographed dances, and even wedding photographs that I take are all unique ways to speak of God's love through beauty. I feel this is especially powerful when artists share their trials and pain as I did in this painting. I know it isn't perfect. But I'll tell you what, I consecrated every brush stroke to Our Lord through Mary. I begged to get out of the way so that Jesus would paint for me. I do this any time I create something. This way, I pray that when anyone looks upon it, they will see truth and love before anything else. I believe this is how we are called to live our daily lives, no matter the task. I fail at this often, but Jesus continues to remind me. He calls us to offer all to him so that everything we do, receive, cultivate, create, give, speaks of him—just as Mary's life models for us.

Painting "The Woman" was extremely vulnerable for me. But I believe that Jesus calls us to give what has been given to us, even and maybe especially the raw, real moments that have the power to bear life in more than just our own lives. I pray that Our Lady of Guadalupe will become a real presence in your life, as she has mine. May you too begin to know her as the truly caring mother that she is, and may we both learn to do as she does, receiving and giving Christ to all.

In joy,

Kate

KATE CAPATO has experienced both the powerful effects of beauty and the cold conditions of its absence. For this reason, she has made beauty her mission. Kate is a sacred art painter, natural light photographer, and contemporary dance choreographer, and she travels worldwide sharing her skills. Kate uses her art to participate in the restoration of our culture and to express the theology of the body and beauty of who we are as man and woman. You can find out more about her art at visualgrace.org.

Nothing is lost or without hope when we give it over to Christ.

Reflection Question and Prayer

"Beauty can come from what seems to be forever lost, through letting our grasp of it go and saying yes to Christ. Dear sister, nothing is lost or without hope when we give it over to Christ. Even huge sins can be made new if we confess and give them over to our heavenly Father and to Mary, our Mother."

How is God revealing himself to you in your life right now? Take a moment to reflect on what you've been reading, watching, and listening to. In even the most unexpected of places—a movie, an article, or a social media post—we can find God's grace and discover something new about his love. What do you think he's revealing to you at this time in your life?

Pray a Hail Mary for the suffering and for those experiencing spiritual isolation. Then, close with this section's petition:

Mary, my Mother and friend, please ask God to grant me the grace to respond to his will with a generous "yes" and to receive his great love for me so that I may share it with others. Amen.

Holiness Over Perfectionism

Dear Sisters,

Three years ago, I heard these words from my doctor: "I want you to know that you're validated. This is a real medical condition, and we're going to get you feeling like yourself again." I had just been diagnosed with a severe depression and anxiety disorder. My husband held my hand as my one-year-old son played with the toys on the floor, oblivious to the magnitude of what was happening around him. When those words rushed over me, the tears came like a flood.

Tears of relief. Tears of pain. Tears of hope.

Those words were ones I had longed to hear for over a year. Why had I waited so long to ask for help? Why did I ignore the signs again and again? In my mind, I was the last person who would ever be diagnosed with depression. Nope not me. I'm happy, normal, and most definitely not crazy. Yet, here I was, crying in a medical office, hearing what I had never wanted to be true.

Before becoming a mother, I had an unrealistic ideal about how a mother should be. The perfect mother never yelled or complained. She was dependable and delightful—a reliable nucleus of warmth, comfort, and beauty. My version of the perfect mother was someone who had the energy of Maria von Trapp, the gentleness of Cinderella, and the homemaking skills of Martha Stewart. Looking back, I realize that I had made an idol of my future family, thinking it would complete my happiness and fulfill me completely.

But after my son came into the world and I was diagnosed with depression, my perfectly designed dreams met the dark reality of living with mental illness. Real life was the opposite of the perfect life I had once daydreamed about as a little girl. I was drowning. I spent hours constantly searching the Internet and parenting books looking for some affirmation that I was enough for my baby. My illness blinded me to my God-given motherly instincts and robbed me of my confidence. I felt suffocated by the weight of the sacrifices expected of me. These days were some of the most painful of my life.

Mental illness is hard to accept and understand. It took a lot of personal growth for me to openly admit that I fall in the "mentally ill" category. But the Lord, in his generosity, has held my hand through it all. By God's grace, my prejudices have been healed, and God has given me the strength to accept this particular cross willingly. I have learned that nothing is ever wasted for God. He uses everything, even the difficult parts of our stories, to bring us closer to him. And this is my story.

On our first Sunday outing as a new family of three, I placed my beautiful one-week-old son in his car seat after Mass. All of a sudden I felt a massive weight on my chest, and I could barely breathe. Immediately after snapping the last buckle on my son's car seat, I collapsed in the church parking lot. My husband rushed over. Seeing the worry written on his face, I laughed it off like it was no big deal. Later, I told my obstetrician about the incident, and she asked me if it could have been a panic attack. A panic attack? No, it couldn't be that. What was there to be anxious about? My doctor ran some tests in case I had a heart condition and monitored me in the months to come, but no physical explanation could be found.

Weeks went by. As a new mom, I was engulfed in the unfamiliar world of diaper changes, sleep deprivation, and painful nursing marathons. On top of all that, we had just moved across the country, and I was away from all of the familiar comforts of home. My husband worked long hours, and I was often left fumbling alone with a newborn. In these days, seeds of resentment grew in me toward my baby. The thought of picking him up when he cried was unbearable. The mere thought of engaging with the world became overwhelming. The heavy weight of the words, "I can't do this anymore," often crept into my mind. There were even moments when I would dream of leaving my son in his crib and driving off, never looking back. I kept hearing an eerie voice in my head saying, "They are better off without you. They deserve so much more than you can give. Look at you, you are a mess! How could they ever love you? God made a mistake when he made you a mother." My only company for most of the day were my own chilling thoughts and a screaming newborn. These thoughts scared me to my core. But still, I said nothing to my friends and family.

As my son's first birthday approached, things went from bad to worse. I spent every unseen moment in my bed crying, aching for some way out of my misery. I was terrified of being left alone. Sometimes, through tears, I would beg my husband to never leave my side and plead with him to stay home from work for the day. Little everyday tasks like leaving the house, cooking dinner, and changing diapers were just too overwhelming. It got to the point that I could not physically do some things. I kept thinking that this must be normal for new mothers. I could not bring myself to acknowledge that I needed help. I felt crippled.

Enslaved to a bleak darkness so encompassing, I knew that relying on Christ alone was the only way to be delivered. On the verge of despair, I made an intentional decision to surrender my pain to the only One who could understand. Every free moment I could, I drove to a nearby adoration chapel to spend time with Our Lord. I sat before Jesus and opened my arms in defeat. I changed my cries from, "Why is this happening to me?" to "Give me the grace to understand why this is happening to me. Give me the strength to carry this burden. I give it to you, Lord."

The main comfort I had during that time was meditating on our Lord's Passion, specifically Jesus' agony in the garden and his receptivity to his salvific mission. I understood for the first time in a real way the isolation and loneliness that Jesus must have experienced as he awaited death on the cross. I found comfort in the abandonment that the Lord experienced because I realized that I could keep him company in *my* darkest moments. I imagined myself keeping watch by Jesus' side in the Garden of Gethsemane. As the Apostles slept (see Mk 14:37), I just sat with Jesus, loving him and weakly praying. I shifted my focus to being thankful—thankful for *his* sacrifice and for allowing me to be a part of it. With this change in the way I thought about my suffering, I realized that the value of my suffering also changed. Now, rather than weigh me down, it could lead me to the heights of sanctity.

By meditating on Jesus' receptivity to his Father's will, I was given the strength to feebly mirror his obedience in my own life. Witnessing Jesus' surrender to the

"In the diversity of peoples who experience the gift of God, each in accordance with its own culture, the Church expresses her genuine catholicity and shows forth the 'beauty of her varied face.'"[41]

—Pope Francis

Father's plan and his example on the cross taught me how to embrace receptivity in my own suffering. I learned how to accept the cross rather than fight it. Once I did, grace came pouring into my heart, and I began to find the courage not only to handle the depression but also the humility to ask for help. This moment was a catalyst of personal transformation. It taught me to view the world with the eyes of my heart. Above all, I have learned that love and mercy must not only extend to those around me but also to myself.

I shudder now when I think back to the days of the darkest thoughts I've ever experienced—thoughts of harming myself or my child in an attempt to escape from my bleak reality. But whenever I remember those moments, I praise God that with his grace I rejected those self-harming thoughts and never entertained them.

Though I found healing through the help of God and medical professionals, I still struggle with depression and anxiety. I've accepted that mental illness is a part of my life right now and therefore is the path the Lord has chosen to bring me to heaven. Just as my vocation as a wife and mother is my path to eternity, so is my cross. My cross is a constant reminder that I am created to be in heaven forever with God, but first I must walk through a valley of tears on earth in order to get there. Like most people, I entered this battle of suffering with clenched teeth and tightly clenched fists only to find out that it did not matter who I was or what I did, I simply could not run from the cross.

What if we always chose to not fight God when suffering comes our way? What if we instead mirrored Jesus' receptivity and accepted the Father's will—the joyful

"Since Christ Himself loved us when we were by no means worthy of love and still loves us with all our unworthiness, our job is to love others without stopping to inquire whether or not they are worthy. That is not our business and, in fact, it is nobody's business. What we are asked to do is to love, and this love itself will render both ourselves and our neighbors worthy."[38]

—Thomas Merton

and the painful too? If acceptance of suffering just seems too difficult, call upon Jesus' Mother. You will find no greater example of feminine receptivity in all of human history than in the moment of the Annunciation. The Blessed Mother Mary's "yes" extended not only to biologically receiving new life but also spiritually as she pondered the weight of God's mission in her heart. By agreeing to bear the Word and to bring him into the world, she unreservedly embraced future emotional suffering as well as her calling to be the mother to all of humanity. We learn from Mary that by reverencing our receptive nature as women, we will ultimately fulfill our individual missions within the tapestry of God's design.

My ideal picture of motherhood and womanhood has changed drastically from that first day in a delivery room four years ago. I now see that the model mother is not a pop-culture celebrity or social media star but a humble handmaid who lived two thousand years ago. When we embrace Mary as our Mother, she instructs us how to boldly reclaim our femininity and model receptivity. Now, the ideal mother for me is a holy mother—a mother who pours her heart into every diaper change, toddler tantrum, and Lego creation; a woman who uses her gifts and her crosses to further glorify God in everything she does, no matter how small. I no longer want to be a perfect mother, I want to be a holy one. A holy mother simply prays and sacrifices, and the more she sacrifices the more she loves. Isn't that our universal calling as Christians no matter our vocation? To love?

I will see you in the Eucharist,

Emily

EMILY FOSSIER is enthusiastic about the small things in life like strong coffee, wildflowers, and uninterrupted naps. She lives on six acres of Louisiana land in an 1850s fixer-upper with her husband and three children. When she is not homeschooling, homemaking, or hiding from her toddlers, she can be found holding hands with her husband as they sip wine on their wraparound porch and dream about renovation projects. Emily, who recently began the six-year discernment process to become a Third Order Carmelite, enjoys studying the writings of Carmelite saints. You can find more about Emily on her blog Little Fossi Way or her Instagram accounts @emilyfossier and @ apostolateofholymotherhood.

"my ideal picture of motherhood and womanhood has changed drastically from that first day in a delivery room four years ago. I now see that the model mother is not a pop-culture celebrity or social media star but a humble handmaid who lived two thousand years ago."

Reflection Question and Prayer

"My version of the perfect mother was someone who had the energy of Maria von Trapp, the gentleness of Cinderella, and the homemaking skills of Martha Stewart. Looking back, I realize that I had made an idol of my future family, thinking it would complete my happiness and fulfill me completely."

Did you grow up with an image of the "perfect woman" in your mind? Reflect on that image. Where did it come from? How has it changed? What is God teaching you about womanhood now?

Pray a Hail Mary for freedom from false images of womanhood and femininity and for those who struggle with mental illness. Then, close with this section's petition:

Mary, my Mother and friend, please ask God to grant me the grace to respond to his will with a generous "yes" and to receive his great love for me so that I may share it with others. Amen.

"When women are able fully to share their gifts with the whole community, the very way in which society understands and organizes itself is improved, and comes to reflect in a better way the substantial unity of the human family. . . . Women have a full right to become actively involved in all areas of public life, and this right must be affirmed and guaranteed."[40]

—Saint John Paul II

An Unexpected Pregnancy

Dear friend,

For as long as I can remember, I've been independent, self-reliant, and resilient. With a mop of curly blonde hair, I didn't need cuddles as a child to feel loved. I thrived in my own self-determination. I know this because of my mother's stories and because I see it now in my daughter.

Becoming a mother challenged me to let myself be loved by God. It began with recognition of my brokenness. After my daughter was born, I realized that her joy relied on my joy, her wholeness on my filled or empty cup, her heart on my broken and healing heart. So this letter is about just that—my heart, my stubborn, little healing heart.

But I am getting ahead of myself. The story that shook my life and taught me love began with a pregnancy test on a February morning in the bathroom of my Los Angeles apartment. I was single and in the process of sending resumes to dream jobs at creative agencies. On weekends, I often would drive—sunroof open—to Malibu and surf. I was finally getting a foothold on the dreamy, golden, sunshine-drenched Los Angeles life I had set out for cross country. And then, in a split second, my future went black.

I still remember what I was wearing as I walked in a daze across the living room. I remember my roommate's expression when she looked up from her wedding plans scattered across the kitchen table. Time stopped as I stood there, staring at a test that read "positive": an earth-shattering challenge to put my selfishness aside

Before I read the result of the test, I had prayed to Mary: "Please, I'm not ready to be a mother." But I knew it was too late. My spiritual life at the time was an endless, exhausting search for meaning and identity—an endeavor made on my own terms. My relationship with God was a constant push and pull. Pull God in when I needed him, push him out when he challenged me to change. I prayed because I wanted to know myself, my purpose, my meaning—yet I was unwilling to sacrifice anything to get there. My appeals to God were selfish. I wanted unconditional love but also to remain in my vices; I made no space for him to transform my heart. I was unwilling to take the plunge, let go of control, hand over the reins, and let him lead. I struggled to trust that God's plan for my life was better than my own.

It took me a week to gather the courage to cancel an appointment for an abortion, despite pressure around me. It took one friend's startling—"You can do it"—across a kitchen countertop for me to drop to my knees and to let hope seep back into my heart. It took one mentor's genuine congratulations—"Alexa, you have a baby inside of you!"—for me to fall into a puddle of tears and embrace the joy I had buried deep inside me in those initial fear-filled days. It took all the courage I could muster to set myself aside and to set out to become love for my unborn child.

The night I made the brave decision to carry out my pregnancy, it was confirmed that I'd most likely be alone on my journey. I would be a single mother. I fell apart with my best friend on the phone. She reminded me of the gravity of my "yes"; certainly, it would come with great pain, but, in time, great joy too. I must have prayed the Joyful Mysteries of the Rosary a hundred times, aching to understand Mary's "yes." *How did you do it? How did you brave the scrutiny? How did you tell your family? How were you so full of trust?*

Soon after, I sat down in a coffee shop to tell a good friend the news. She was one of the most difficult people to tell because she was also pregnant—six months to be exact. I was so afraid of the judgment I would face. When her husband kissed her on the cheek as he left us alone, all I could feel was unbearable shame, *She did it the right way*. But then I told her—and joy filled the coffee shop. My friend hugged me, her bulging belly resting again my flat stomach. I broke down in tears as I remembered the scene of the Magnificat: Elizabeth's excitement upon seeing Mary; a child leaping in her womb. I realized that Mary was there with me, celebrating my "yes." In my fear, God was holding me close to my friends and wrapping his arms around me.

I started to feel God's love wrap around my life in a way I hadn't ever felt before. I began to let myself feel love for the first time. Throughout my painful and stress-filled pregnancy, I began to go to God in prayer. I'd close my eyes, focus on my breath and ask him to let me sit in his presence. Each time, God showed me that love existed all around me. He showed me the moments during my childhood when he was there, beaming with joy at my existence. The moments when I carelessly gave pieces of my heart away and was full of shame. He was always there, his arms wrapped around me as I wept in my emptiness. Slowly, God asked me to hand him every piece of my aching and broken heart. He asked me to let each piece go, to give them up and to quit clinging to my brittle imperfection. Instead, he asked me to let myself be loved by him in all of my humanness. It was the most difficult metamorphosis I've ever been invited into. But I did it because I knew I needed healing before I could bring a sweet, innocent person into the world.

The day my daughter Renley was born, I felt peaceful but still emotionally unprepared. My contractions began at 7 a.m., and more than seven hours later, the doctor told me it was time to push. Suddenly, I was filled with anxiety. After a pregnancy filled with heartache, stress, and emotion, I was worried that I wasn't ready to meet her. *What kind of mother would I be? What if I wouldn't be able to hold it together? How could I be strong for this little one when I still felt like I was crumbling?* And then I thought of my journey—the hope I'd experienced amid hopelessness, the pain words couldn't express, and the joy peeking through at the same time. I remembered the gravity of my continuous "yes." So, just as I had pushed myself forward a little each day for nine months, I pushed.

Then the doctor said, "Reach down and grab her!" and I looked into my daughter's eyes for the very first time. That was joy. The girl I'd carried for ten months. Even in my sorrow and anger, I'd carried her. And I knew all along that someday she'd carry me, that she'd lift me up. As I pulled her to my chest, time stopped. But this time without fear. In that moment, I experienced the most raw, life-giving love I have ever experienced. I must have kissed her a thousand times through joy-filled tears. Over and over again, I whispered, "You're perfect." And I now know what I meant: *this is perfect love.*

My journey of learning how to receive love didn't stop the day my daughter was born. It still hasn't. One day when I was nursing Renley, she looked up at me in total dependence with the most loving gaze I'd ever seen. Tears streamed down my face as I realized that this must be how the Father looks at me: with loving eyes and a forgiving heart. A heart that carries no contingencies or expectations. The kind of look that says, "I love you because you are mine, and that is all. You are *enough.*" And in the same breath, I realized I had never once looked at myself with the same kind of love.

From that day forward, I began to try to see myself that way. Flawed but beautiful. Broken but healing. A beacon of light amid darkness—if only I would just let myself be light. I focused on gratitude and all the little things I was accomplishing. Each night as I brushed my teeth, I pinned my accomplishments on my bathroom mirror. I stopped measuring my worth by my productivity and started accepting my new limitations. Gradually, my anxiety slowed. I moved in with my parents and picked up each piece of my broken heart, slowly stitching it anew.

Now, I'm a full-time working, single mother navigating the wilderness of raising a toddler in a two-bedroom Chicago apartment. Though Renley's father is involved, it is often confusing parenting alone, but I'm surrounded by a strong support system: my parents, my nanny (my angel), my sister (my roomie), my grandparents, my wonderful boss and mentor, supportive people who come out of the woodwork, and my best friends whom I call and confide in daily. I deal with the challenges of motherhood in a variety of ways: with sweatpants and happy music to shake off work mode and ease into mom mode; hot bubble baths to the tune of Etta James and Julie London; fifteen minutes of daily meditative prayer that have drastically altered my life.

I listen to my gut. I pray through every big decision. I focus on trust and I let God show me the big picture. I still brave difficult seasons, but now I do it with my hands open instead of with stubborn clenched fists. I trust that God is taking me one step deeper, that I'm shedding a layer of skin that needs shedding. I trust that something is happening, and there's good in the happening, even if I'm stretched beyond my comfort zone. I trust that I'm not alone on my journey.

Motherhood threw me into a whirlwind of growth and literal rebirth. I suppose maybe in order for me to fully understand love, I had to see and touch it. That's just stubborn old me. Renley was my light amid darkness, the smiley face and curly red hair into which I bury my nose every morning. To fully understand the love I was lacking, I had to witness love in the eyes of a person who came directly from me. And with that, my identity as a woman shifted. As I moved through that valley of darkness, I came to see my own grace and resilience. As a woman who never once daydreamed of children or thought she'd be a great mother, I embraced my feminine ability to nurture. Experiencing difficulty was my way to empathy. The sacrificial life of motherhood turned me inside out, but it also taught me how to reach out rather than inward. I realized more than ever that we women *need* each other. Becoming a mother made me a better friend, daughter, and sister. More than that, it cut me down at the knees and begged me, *Be a better woman—for yourself, for your daughter, for the one who created you.*

My journey of learning to love myself and receive love began *back in February.* But I know now that loving myself as a woman didn't need to begin with the birth of my child. Loving ourselves as women begins with recognition of our brokenness and asking God to love us in all of it. Loving ourselves comes with the difficulty of keeping our hands open, of consciously letting go of control, and of trusting that something greater than ourselves exists. Loving ourselves comes with recognizing that we were uniquely created, so carefully formed in beauty and femininity that we each cannot be replicated. When we clench our hands and clutch our own ideas of happiness, we decline to receive something so much greater than our human imagination can fathom.

For so much of my life, my heart tried to thrive in darkness; I relied on my own imperfect self to be my own light. But as it turns out, light begets light. Love begets love. Open hands beget *receiving.* If only we would run to the source of all those things.

xoxo,

Alexa

ALEXA HYMAN is a full-time working mother who lives in Chicago with her two-year-old daughter, Renley Jane. She is a writer, contributor, and bubble-bath lover. After experiencing an unplanned pregnancy, Alexa became passionate about sharing her personal experience to help other women feel less alone. When she is not working in financial services, she mentors women facing unplanned pregnancies. You can find her on Instagram at @backinfebruary_ or at BackinFebruary.com.

My journey of learning to
love myself and receive love
began back in February. But
I know now, that loving myself
as a woman didn't need to
begin with the birth of my child.

   Loving ourselves as women
begins with recognition of our
brokenness and asking God to
love us in _all_ of it.

                    Alisa

Reflection Question and Prayer

"Loving ourselves as women begins with recognition of our brokenness and asking God to love us in all of it. Loving ourselves comes with the difficulty of keeping our hands open, of consciously letting go of control, and of trusting that something greater than ourselves exists. . . . When we clench our hands and clutch our own ideas of happiness, we decline to receive something so much greater than our human imagination can fathom."

Take a moment to reflect on the sins you find yourself struggling with the most and consider their origins. What false "ideas of happiness" do you tend to clutch? How might your struggles with different sins be related? Ask the Holy Spirit to help you to understand why you struggle with these sins and for the grace to be able to let them go and to find healing and wholeness in God.

Then, pray a Hail Mary for women facing unexpected pregnancies, that they may find God's love and peace. Finally, close with this section's petition:

Mary, my Mother and friend, please ask God to grant me the grace to respond to his will with a generous "yes" and to receive his great love for me so that I may share it with others. Amen.

Broken Plans,
Open Heart

Dear friend,

I have always had a plan.

I knew what I wanted to study, what I wanted to do. I knew when I would marry, when my kids would be born. I knew exactly what life would hold.

I love plans.

Of course, I ought to have known that my big plans wouldn't go exactly as I imagined. But no worries: I also love little plans. I love knowing what a day will bring. I love mapping out the conversations I expect to have later and even daydreaming about grocery shopping. I love the control that comes with having a plan. Even when things are derailed, I just put another plan in place; I piece together the things that can be salvaged and toss the rest.

And so—because God is good—I have no plan.

I don't know where I'll be next month. I don't know where I'll be next Tuesday. Sometimes I have a pretty good sense of how the next six months will look—until things suddenly shift, and I'm trying to figure out where I'm going to spend the night.

For the last seven years, I've been living out of my car. I'm a missionary, traveling the world to tell people about God's extravagant love. I sleep in strangers' houses and drive fifteen hours at a stretch. I speak at huge conferences and intimate gatherings, and I have very little control over any of it. If you told me ten years ago that this would be my life, I would have laughed derisively or had a panic attack.

How on earth does a type-A, control freak wander aimlessly for years? It started, as the best adventures do, in the chapel. Or, rather, it started when I realized that I needed to spend time each day in chapel. Not just for Mass, or a Rosary, or *lectio divina*, but for silence. Real, awkward, exhausting, uncomfortable silence. Every day. I wasn't thrilled. Sure, I had sat in silence before the tabernacle when I had something to say. Or, more frequently, something to demand. But every day? For half an hour? Without a single thing to distract me? *Oof.*

Still, I knew that saints are formed in the crucible of silence, and I want to be a saint. So I committed to that silence, to those interminable minutes of boredom, frustration, and half-waking dreams so rarely interrupted by a moment of clarity, peace, or understanding.

And God began to speak. Not audibly. Not in any visible way. But things started to become clear. As I sat and stared at the tabernacle, day in and day out, God began to form my heart. And, improbably, my heart was longing to quit the teaching job I loved, to move into my car, and to start wandering. A terrible idea. But, somehow, it didn't seem like one.

Somehow, in the hours of silence, the Lord had started to till the soil of my heart so that I could receive him. He didn't shout, he didn't even murmur. He just drew me on, making me desire what I normally wouldn't desire: a life with no plan. So I quit my job and moved into my car, leaving behind a baffled school and town community. But I knew that this no-plan life was what God wanted, so I went.

Unsurprisingly, I've found that I'm not very good at living without plans. Just because I don't have a ten-year plan (or even ten-month plan) doesn't mean I don't cling to control over my day-to-day. I try to trust, I really do. But it is so easy, even in a life that looked surrendered, to try to take control.

Mercifully, God loves me too much to leave me to my own devices. In his deep love for me, he busts my master cylinder. He cancels my flight. He sends my friend into labor at just the wrong time. My plans are ruined, adjusted, accepted, and ruined again. Always for good reasons: a soul needs to be loved, a woman needs to pour out her broken heart, a man needs someone to pray with him.

Sometimes, just when my plans fall apart, I am met with pure gift. Once, when my car broke down, a stranger bought me a plane ticket. In Istanbul, when I had no place to stay while rioting filled the streets and the city was under martial law, I was invited to stay the night in a convent. More often than not, God shows me how my odd and inconvenient circumstances lead me to people who needed to be seen and loved.

Once, for some reason, I decided to *drive* from Texas to Chicago to save twenty bucks on a plane ticket to Alaska. Now, this was not my first rodeo. I knew it didn't make any sense to drive seventeen hours to save a few dollars. But I gave God those precious minutes in silence each day, so when this illogical itinerary made sense, I took it not as penny-pinching insanity but as a prompting of the Spirit. I bought the ticket out of Chicago. I waited. I wondered. Then, a few days before my trip, I spontaneously texted a girlfriend in Chicago to ask if we could visit a bit before I flew out.

When I arrived at my friend's house, we chatted for some time. After she put her kids to bed, my friend looked at me seriously. With an expression that made it clear this wasn't (yet) a joyful announcement, she said, "I'm pregnant." I gasped and simultaneously congratulated and commiserated with this exhausted, working mom who hadn't been planning on yet another baby.

"The other day, when I took the test, I wanted to talk to you," my friend said. "I thought, 'Meg would understand. She'd be so happy about this baby, but she'd also understand that this is hard. I wish I could talk to Meg.'" I understand why she didn't call; we're not that kind of friends, the kind you call on the phone when something's tough—the kind you call on the phone ever. We're love-you-so-hard-when-I'm-in-your-living-room friends.

"And then," she said, "You texted me. Right then. And asked if you could come stay."

Ah. I see. That's why I drove to Chicago to fly to Alaska. So I could be with her.

Once I waited until the very last minute to ask a friend if I could visit, only to discover that the moment before I texted, she had prayed that God would send her someone to talk to. Another time when my plans were canceled, I stayed the night with a woman I had met only once years before. After dinner, she looked at me and said, "Today has been the worst day of my life."

Ah. I see.

Again and again, a dozen stories, a hundred moments, a thousand times I've made a choice (or had one made for me) that put me in the path of a broken heart that needed to be held. I'm not, by nature, a good listener. Not in prayer, not to lectures, not to people's problems. I'm distracted and focused on what I'm going to do or say next. I'm a planner. But God has asked me to sit before him and receive. And every day, as I try to stay awake through my Holy Hour, he tills the soil of my heart. He prepares me to receive his promptings, his guidance—him. He's also giving me a heart ready to receive the brokenness of his darlings. By his grace, I've become a woman who listens, a woman who rejoices with those who rejoice and weeps with those who weep. I spend less time preparing my response and more time just being a safe place for suffering souls to share.

There's something so profoundly maternal about the receptivity that God's been nurturing in me, something so deeply feminine. Most people he puts in front of me don't need advice or a solution to their problems. They want to be listened to, loved, and held. They don't need me to fix anything, they just need me to be there. It's enough that I make space for them (or accept the canceled plans through which God makes that space) and take them into my heart.

Now, there's nothing wrong with being a planner—if you hold your plans with open hands and allow the will of God (or the needs of others) to lead you in a different direction when necessary. But for someone whose fists are often clenched tight around her plans, ideas, and demands, it has been a great relief to have my aching fingers so gently pried open. Through seemingly fruitless hours of prayer, my plans have been pushed aside so that I can receive God's plans, so that I can receive God's people.

This is the call of the Christian life and my deepest longing: to have a heart open to receive God's will in such a transformative way that his people find a home in us. May he break our hearts, if necessary, so that his love can enter in.

Yours in the pierced Heart of Jesus,

Meg

MEG HUNTER-KILMER is a hobo missionary. After receiving two theology degrees from Notre Dame and working for five years as a high school religion teacher, she quit her job in 2012 to live out of her car and preach the Gospel to anyone who would listen. Fifty states and twenty-five countries later, this seems to have been a less ridiculous decision than she initially thought. Meg blogs at piercedhands.com and aleteia.org, and she posts regularly on Instagram and Facebook.

This is the call of the Christian heart and my deepest longing: to have a heart open to receive God's will in such a transformative way that his people find a home in us.

Reflection Question and Prayer

"There's something so profoundly maternal about the receptivity that God's been nurturing in me, something so deeply feminine. Most people he puts in front of me don't need advice or a solution to their problems. They want to be listened to, loved, and held. They don't need me to fix anything, they just need me to be there. It's enough that I make space for them (or accept the canceled plans through which God makes that space) and take them into my heart."

Reflect on the moments you interact with others throughout the day. How do you typically react when you're interrupted? Do you tend to treat the person as a problem to be solved, or do you try to listen? In the future, what are little ways you can practice the act of being present to others in your everyday life? How is God calling you to let go of your plans and to be a "home" for and with others today?

Pray a Hail Mary for all those whose plans have been broken by tragedy and loss. Then, close with this section's petition:

Mary, my Mother and friend, please ask God to grant me the grace to respond to his will with a generous "yes" and to receive his great love for me so that I may share it with others. Amen.

Write Your Own Letter

Dearest Reader,

We hope these letters have been as inspirational for you as they were for us. We belong to such an old, expansive, beautiful Church that so many different women have called home throughout the centuries—a Church in which every woman is called to love and invite others, through her own unique, God-given gifts and feminine presence, into a place where they can truly belong. As you finish this book, we want to invite you to write your own letter to a woman in your life. It could be for your best friend, your mother, a mentor, your daughter or any other woman who has changed your life for the better. Maybe it's a woman who has inspired you in your faith at one point along your journey, or perhaps it's a close friend who has fallen away from the Church and is in need of love. Take some time to pray about it. Before writing your letter, ask God how you can show his love for the person to whom you are writing, through your letter. Though you are welcome to write whatever you'd like, we highly recommend taking time in your letter to share concretely how the recipient of your letter has impacted your life and why you are grateful for her.

Thanks again,

Corynne and The Catholic Woman Team

I BELIEVE
IN GOD THE FATHER
ALMIGHTY MAKER OF
HEAVEN AND EARTH:
AND IN JESUS CHRIST
HIS ONLY SON OUR LORD
WHO WAS CONCEIVED
BY THE HOLY GHOST
BORN OF THE VIRGIN
MARY, SUFFERED UNDER
PONTIUS PILATE WAS
CRUCIFIED DEAD AND
BURIED. HE DESCENDED
INTO HELL: THE THIRD
DAY HE ROSE AGAIN FROM
THE DEAD. HE ASCENDED
INTO HEAVEN AND SITTETH
ON THE RIGHT HAND OF GOD
THE FATHER ALMIGHTY:
FROM THENCE HE SHALL
COME TO JUDGE THE QUICK
AND THE DEAD.
BELIEVE IN THE HOLY
GHOST, THE HOLY CATHOLIC
CHURCH: THE
COMMUNION OF SAINTS:
THE FORGIVENESS OF SINS:
THE RESURRECTION
AND THE LIFE

Acknowledgments

This book would not exist were it not for the support, effort, and encouragement of countless people. It's impossible to thank them all, but I would like to give thanks to as many as I can. First, thank you to the writers featured in this book for vulnerably and courageously sharing your stories! Many of your letters are already transforming the way I treat others, the way I understand God, and how I make sense of my own life as a Catholic woman. To each of the writers: I am extremely honored to be sharing some of your story with the rest of the world. Thank you again.

Additionally, I want to thank Saint Cecilia Parish in Cincinnati, Ohio for allowing me to take photos in their beautiful parish, and Sarah, Maria, Hannah, Grace, Maricris, and Renessa for modeling for many of the pictures included in this book.

I'm so grateful to our team at The Catholic Woman—thank you for bringing our mission to life. I'm thankful to be working with each of you. Thank you for volunteering your time, passion, and gifts to serve the Church in this unique way. And a big thank you to The Catholic Woman donors for supporting our mission. You have played an instrumental part in bringing this book to life. Without your generosity, this book would not exist.

Thank you to the Daughters of St. Paul and Pauline Books & Media for seeing the need for this book and for believing in its vision. I'm honored to have worked with each of you. Truly, this has been a blast. And to Sister Theresa Aletheia Noble, FSP: several of our conversations, including my interviews with you for The Catholic Woman, played a large role in the inspiration for this book. I honestly can't think of another person I'd rather have editing this project. Thanks for being a part of this.

I'm also infinitely grateful for the support of my parents. To Mom and Dad: thank you for raising me to know and to love Jesus in such a personal, intimate, and fearless way—something that I think is quite rare. Thank you for your encouragement and for your advice while I created this book. You both inspire me in your own ways. I love you both. And to the Staresinics: thank you for your kindness, your festive hospitality, and your enthusiastic support. I'm grateful to have you both in my life. Love you guys—cheers to you!

And finally, thanks to Nick and Eloise. To El: my girl. If you ever read this book, I hope it brings you peace in who you are and hope in eternity. In a certain sense, this is all for you, really. I love you, kid. To Nick: much like the rest of my life, this book would be a lot worse without your love, kind constructive criticism, and killer sense of humor. Thanks for editing my writing several times over, for believing in me, and for telling me to laugh when I missed one of your jokes. Finally, thanks for taking care of El so I could work on this book, for staying up late to keep me company, and for making me meals and drinks to celebrate the mile-markers. Nick, you're the best friend I've ever had. Love you forever.

Credits

Notes

1. Pope John Paul II, *Mulieris Dignitatem* (Vatican: 1988), no. 24, http://www.vatican.va/content/john-paul-ii/en/apost_letters/1988/documents/hf_jp-ii_apl_19880815_mulieris-dignitatem.html.

2. Pope John Paul II, *Letter to Women* (Vatican: 1994), nos. 3, 10, http://www.vatican.va/content/john-paul-ii/en/letters/1995/documents/hf_jp-ii_let_29061995_women.html.

3. Edith Stein, *Essays on Women: The Collected Works of Edith Stein*, vol. 2, trans. Freda Mary Oben (Washington, D.C.: ICS Publications, 1996), 49.

4. Edith Stein, *Self-Portrait in Letters: 1916–1942*, trans. Josephine Koeppel (Washington, D.C.: ICS Publications, 1994), 281.

5. *Kristallnacht* (meaning "Night of Broken Glass") refers to a wave of violent, anti-Jewish attacks that took place on November 9 and 10, 1938, throughout Germany and several other countries. The violence resulted in shattered glass from windows of synagogues, homes, and Jewish-owned businesses that was scattered in German streets. — *Ed.*

6. See Edith Stein, *Self-Portrait in Letters*, 296.

7. Teresia Renata Posselt, O.C.D., *Edith Stein: The Life of a Philosopher and Carmelite* (Washington, DC: ICS Publications, 2012), https://www.google.com/books/edition/Edith_Stein_the_Life_of_a_Philosopher_an/0V0zrkEKhsMC?hl=en&gb-pv=1&bsq=Among%20the%20prisoners%20.

8. Edith Stein, *Essays*, 54.

9. Ibid., 264.

10. Dorothy Day, *The Long Loneliness: The Autobiography of the Legendary Catholic Social Activist* (San Francisco: HarperOne, 2009), 285.

11. Pietro Molla, *Saint Gianna Molla: Wife, Mother, Doctor* (San Francisco: Ignatius Press, 2004), https://books.google.com/books?id=jcJHDwAAQBAJ&q=sun#v=snippet&q=sun&f=false.

12. Charles W. Elliot, ed., *Blaise Pascal, Volume 48 of Harvard Classics* (New York: P.F. Collier & Son, 1910), 98.

13. Sr. Prudence Allen, RSM, *Concept of a Woman*, vol. 1 (Grand Rapids: William B. Eerdmans Publishing Company, 1985), 295.

14. Pope Benedict XVI, *General Audience* (Vatican: Wednesday, 8 September 2010), http://www.vatican.va/content/benedict-xvi/en/audiences/2010/documents/hf_ben-xvi_aud_20100908.html.

15. Jacques-Paul Migne, *Patrologiae latina cursus completus . . . series secunda* (Aqud Editorem, 1855). https://books.google.com/books?id=dJ5BAAAAcAAJ&pg=PA217&lpg=PA217&dq=%22Audi,+o+sollicita+filia,+quia+homines+istos+quos+inspiratio.

16. Pope John Paul II, *Letter to Artists* (The Vatican: 1999), no. 2 http://www.vatican.va/content/john-paul-ii/en/letters/1999/documents/hf_jp-ii_let_23041999_artists.html.

17. Pope Benedict XVI, *Meeting with Artists* (Vatican: 2009) http://w2.vatican.va/content/benedict-xvi/en/speeches/2009/november/documents/hf_ben-xvi_spe_20091121_artisti.html.

18. Ibid.

19. Jean Baptise Pitra, *Analecta sacra spicilegio solesmensi parata* (Paris: A. Jouby et Roger, 1882), 556.

20. Though Jesus taught us to call God "Father," the practice of referring to God's maternal aspects is also rooted in Scripture. The *Catechism of the Catholic Church* explains: "By calling God 'Father', the language of faith indicates two main things: that God is the first origin of everything and transcendent authority; and that he is at the same time goodness and loving care for all his children. God's parental tenderness can also be expressed by the image of motherhood, which emphasizes God's immanence, the intimacy between Creator and creature . . . The language of faith thus draws on the human experience of parents, who are in a way the first representatives of God for man. But this experience also tells us that human parents are fallible and can disfigure the face of fatherhood and motherhood. We ought therefore to recall that God transcends the human distinction between the sexes" (239). —*Ed.*

21. John Paul II, *Mulieris*, no.19.

22. Regine Pernoud, *The Retrial of Joan of Arc: The Evidence of Her Vindication*, trans. J.M. Cohen (San Francisco: Ignatius Press, 2007), 93.

23. Pope Francis, *Mass, Imposition of the Pallium and Bestowal of the Fisherman's Ring for the Beginning of the Petrine Ministry of the Bishop of Rome* (Vatican: 2013), http://www.vatican.va/content/francesco/en/homilies/2013/documents/papa-francesco_20130319_omelia-inizio-pontificato.html.

24. Francis M. Kalvelage, *Kolbe: Saint of the Immaculata* (San Francisco: Ignatius Press: 2002), 31.

25. United States Conference of Catholic Bishops, *Called to Global Solidarity International Challenges for US Parishes* (Washington, D.C.: USCCB, 1997), The Demands of Solidarity, http://www.usccb.org/issues-and-action/human-life-and-dignity/global-issues/called-to-global-solidarity-international-challenges-for-u-s-parishes.cfm.

26. Pope John Paul II, *Centesimus Annus* (Vatican: 1991), no. 51, http://www.vatican.va/content/john-paul-ii/en/encyclicals/documents/hf_jp-ii_enc_01051991_centesimus-annus.html.

27. Mother Teresa, *Where There Is Love, There Is God: Her Path to Closer Union with God and Greater Love for Others* (New York: Image Books, 2012), 330.

28. Helen Alvare and Mary Rice Hasson, "Even Our Feminism Must Be Service," in *Promise and Challenge: Catholic Women Reflect on Feminism, Complementarity, and the Church* (Huntington, IN: Our Sunday Visitor, 2015), https://books.google.com/books?id=K3T8CwAAQBAJ&pg=PT17&dq=Even+Our+Feminism+Must+Be+Service&hl=en&newbks=1&newbks_redir=0&sa=X&ved=2ahUKEwiCreKn9LroAh-WEVc0KHUfPBW0Q6AEwAHoECAMQAg#v=onepage&q=I%20SUBMIT%20THAT&f=false.

29. Pope Francis, *Laudato Si* (Vatican: 2015), no. 49, http://www.vatican.va/content/francesco/en/encyclicals/documents/papa-francesco_20150524_enciclica-laudato-si.html.

30. Pope John Paul II, *Letter to Women* (The Vatican: 1995), no. 10, http://www.vatican.va/content/john-paul-ii/en/letters/1995/documents/hf_jp-ii_let_29061995_women.html.

31. Pope John Paul II, *Apostolic Journey to the Czech Republic: Mass for the Youth.* April 26, 1997. https://w2.vatican.va/content/john-paul-ii/en/homilies/1997/documents/hf_jp-ii_hom_19970426.html.

32. Blessed Raymond of Capua, *The Life of St. Catherine of Siena*, (Dublin: James Duffy and Co., 1901?) 323, http://www.saintsbooks.net/books/Bl.%20Raymund%20of%20Capua%20-%20The%20Life%20of%20St.%20Catherine%20of%20Siena.pdf.

33. Pope Benedict XVI, *General Audience* (Vatican: Wednesday, 24 November 2010), http://www.vatican.va/content/benedict-xvi/en/audiences/2010/documents/hf_ben-xvi_aud_20101124.html.

34. Ibid.

35. Day, *The Long Loneliness*, 286.

36. Pope John Paul II, *Letter of His Holiness John Paul II to Mrs. Gertrude Mongella* (The Vatican: 1995), no. 6, http://www.vatican.va/content/john-paul-ii/en/letters/1995/documents/hf_jp-ii_let_19950526_mongella-pechino.html.

37. Saint Gregory of Nazianzus, Oration 43 from *Nicene and Post-Nicene Fathers*, Second Series, Vol. 7. Edited by Philip Schaff and Henry Wace. (Buffalo, NY: Christian Literature Publishing Co., 1894). Translated by Charles Gordon Browne and James Edward Swallow. Revised and edited for New Advent by Kevin Knight. http://www.newadvent.org/fathers/310243.htm.

38. Thomas Merton, *Disputed Questions* (Boston: Houghton Mifflin Harcourt, 1985), 125.

39. Karol Wojtyla, *Love and Responsibility, trans. Grzegorz Ignatik (Boston: Pauline Books & Media, 2013), 25.*

40. Pope John Paul II, *Women: Teachers of Peace* (Vatican: 1995), no. 9, http://www.vatican.va/content/john-paul-ii/en/messages/peace/documents/hf_jp-ii_mes_08121994_xxviii-world-day-for-peace.html.

41. Pope Francis, *Evangeli Gaudium* (Vatican: 2013), no. 116, http://www.vatican.va/content/francesco/en/apost_exhortations/documents/papa-francesco_esortazione-ap_20131124_evangelii-gaudium.html.

If you have enjoyed this book, check out The Catholic Woman, a nonprofit dedicated to inspiring millennial Catholic women to live their faith. We do this by illustrating the many faces and callings of women in the Church through different mediums, including letters, videos, and interviews with different Catholic women. You can find an archive of letters, similar to what you've found here, from Catholic women of all walks of life on our website: www.thecatholicwoman.co. We're always looking for new stories to share, so if you have one or know a Catholic woman we should reach out to for a letter, film, or interview series, please connect with us through our website. We hope you consider sharing your witness in this way. Finally, if this book has made a positive impact on your life, we also would sincerely love to hear from you through our website.

 **Corynne Staresinic** is the founder and director of The Catholic Woman, a nonprofit multimedia platform dedicated to fostering a sense of belonging among Catholic women. Corynne is passionate about exploring the meaning of womanhood and the many different ways Catholic women live out the call to holiness. She is a convert to Catholicism from Evangelicalism and lives in the Cincinnati-Northern Kentucky area with her husband and kids.

BOOKS & MEDIA

A mission of the Daughters of St. Paul

As apostles of Jesus Christ, evangelizing today's world:

We are CALLED to holiness
by God's living Word and Eucharist.

We COMMUNICATE the Gospel message
through our lives and through all
available forms of media.

We SERVE the Church
by responding to the hopes and needs
of all people with the Word of God,
in the spirit of St. Paul.

For more information visit us at www.pauline.org.

BOOKS & MEDIA

The Daughters of St. Paul operate book and media centers at the following addresses. Visit, call, or write the one nearest you today, or find us at www.paulinestore.org.

CALIFORNIA
3908 Sepulveda Blvd, Culver City, CA 90230   310-397-8676
3250 Middlefield Road, Menlo Park, CA 94025   650-562-7060

FLORIDA
145 S.W. 107th Avenue, Miami, FL 33174   305-559-6715

HAWAII
1143 Bishop Street, Honolulu, HI 96813   808-521-2731

ILLINOIS
172 North Michigan Avenue, Chicago, IL 60601   312-346-4228

LOUISIANA
4403 Veterans Memorial Blvd, Metairie, LA 70006   504-887-7631

MASSACHUSETTS
885 Providence Hwy, Dedham, MA 02026   781-326-5385

MISSOURI
9804 Watson Road, St. Louis, MO 63126   314-965-3512

NEW YORK
115 E. 29th Street, New York City, NY 10016   212-754-1110

SOUTH CAROLINA
243 King Street, Charleston, SC 29401   843-577-0175

VIRGINIA
1025 King Street, Alexandria, VA 22314   703-549-3806

CANADA
3022 Dufferin Street, Toronto, ON M6B 3T5   416-781-9131